The First Jew

THE FIRST JEW

Prejudice and Politics in an American Community, 1900-1932

Richard Klayman

Old Suffolk Square Press
Malden, Massachusetts

Library of Congress Cataloging in Publication Data
Klayman, Richard.
    The first Jew.

    Bibliography: p.
    Includes index.
    1. Jews—Massachusetts—Malden—History.   2. Antisemi-
tism—Massachusetts—Malden.   3. Malden (Mass.)—
Ethnic relations.   I. Title.
F74.M2K57 1985   974.4'4   84-62452
ISBN 0-932247-00-8

Table of Contents

Preface

How did you ever get there?

What was life like for you there?

These two questions have a special significance to almost any religious or ethnic minority who has lived outside an ancestral home. These questions have a special importance to Jews who, until recent times, lived in a condition of Diaspora, everywhere alien to a somewhat native or indigenous population. In fact, these two questions embody a fundamental link or bond that unites the most disparate of ethnic people, irrespective of geographical location.

In a sense, this book is about the cross fertilization of cultures that distinguishes our American civilization. It is the story of Jewish life and Irish life in a small American city at the beginning of the twentieth century, with the expectations of a new century before them. The city in which the story takes place, Malden, was and remains a small city in eastern Massachusetts that serves as a metaphor both within the time and illustratively, of the scope of that new century.

Clearly, this study calls for the recognition of first generation Americans as contributing to an evolving American political culture within the multitude of cities, towns, and villages that experienced an ethnic infusion, especially in the first few decades of the twentieth century.

In this study of one city, it remains my hope that similar studies will explore the local ethnic condition, especially those that comment upon or help us understand the cutting edge of social and political change within the greater America.

It remains also a goal of this work that American ethnic history will not foresake the lowly or the common, the unheralded and the largely forgotten masses of American immigrants. There must be a blending, therefore, of quantitative history with a more traditional or narrative history to accurately and engagingly make the American political and intellectual record more telling.

A few words concerning the book's title, *The First Jew*. When I began the research for this book, I was struck by a paradox in the literature of American ethnic and political history. On the one hand, scholars suggested that first generation Americans possessed little in the way of political consciousness and, thus, were out of the American political mainstream, particularly as regards participation in social reform movements. East European Jews, for example, were said to be more concerned with those aspects of "making a living" and "making a life" than with voting or discerning America's political system. Without examining the American Jewish voting record to any satisfactory degree, such a generalization troubled me.

The rather extensive literature regarding anti-Semitism and social history appeared to confirm on the other hand that the presence of East European Jewry had quite an unsettling effect upon twentieth century urban America, especially as regards social and cultural change. In America's smaller cities, I wondered, had the Jewish presence precipitated a "culture shock" without any related or comparable "political shock"? As my research in the politics and social life of a single city developed, it became increasingly clear that

American Jews looked upon American politics as alien but inherently part of their new lives, doubtless, owing to the Jewish commitment that each individual must work to improve the framework of everyday life. In fact, the Jewish dedication to *real* and *substantive* change put American Jews, by definition, in the forefront of those political efforts to reshape America's social fabric. While American Jews may not have been prominent in the leadership of certain social reform movements, American Jews voted with evident persistency for social reform. It was evident very early in my research that the small city Jew was clearly, in fact, associated with the tumult of political and social change, and that the presence of the Jew was, at least symbolically, a measuring rod in understanding when the "old America" gave way to the "new America". As such, the first Jew became both a symbol and a bellwether of when Malden and all America underwent a most profound transformation.

Many people and institutions made this project possible. My thanks to the staffs and agency heads of the City of Malden, especially the Office of the Clerk, Office of the Assessor, the Malden Police Department, and the Malden Engineering Department. The librarians and staff of the Malden Public Library, the Malden Historical Society, The Suffolk Square Reunion Society, The American Jewish Archives, The American Jewish Historical Society, the Boston Public Library, and Bunker Hill Community College Library were courteous, patient and most helpful. David Brickman, editor of the *Malden Evening News*, encouraged the project from its inception, as did Lawrence Harmon of *The Jewish Advocate*.

My bibliography recognizes many of those scholars to whom I owe a very special debt, above and beyond this manuscript. The extraordinary talents of Richard Abrams, Moses Rischin, Robert

Wiebe, Irving Howe, and, of course, Oscar Handlin have inspired historians such as myself, albeit exclusively through their writing.

On a more personal level, I have benefited from many excellent teachers and scholars. Dr. Peter Siegle possesses a sense of American-Jewish life that is sensitive, and full of wisdom and insight. Dr. Robert Mennel of the University of New Hampshire was a patient and thoughtful teacher who labored to demonstrate to an often doubting student the analytical potential of quantitative history. His lectures were not in vain.

My wife Nancy encouraged me and supported me in ways too numerous to mention. Our home life always included the time to question and discuss the American ethnic experience because of our mutual and deep commitment to all that ethnic America represents. And it would be quite remiss not to mention that my wife helped financially to sustain our family so that this book would be realized. And yet she, beyond all others, understands that this book is dedicated to our children, Andrea and Lauren.

For Lauren & Andrea

The First Jew

Introduction

"The Mill Pond Gleams No More"

The family of Malden's first sexton or *shammes*, 1906

The small American city offers a unique vantage point from which to interpret America's ethnic legacy. As the historian J. Joseph Huthmacher noted some two decades ago, small town America was brimming with archives and libraries untapped by historical inquiry. And especially for research regarding the lives of first generation Americans in the 1900-1930 era, small towns and cities maintained a plethora of local and ethnic news papers, extant voting records, memoirs, and organizational records, that, undoubtedly lacked the "glamour" of more prestigious archives or libraries, but were treasure chests in the examination of American politics and society.[1]

Published in 1959, *Massachusetts' People and Politics, 1919-1933*, was Huthmacher's study of voting returns and political activities of lower class urban peoples, especially the relatively ensconced Irish as well as "newer" immigrant groups, including Jews, Poles, and Italians who poured into the factories, textile mills, and other light industrial workshops that were a part of so many of Massachusetts' three hundred and one cities and towns. Huthmacher suggested that lower class immigrants, throughout Massachusetts and probably throughout urban America, philosophically embraced and cast their votes for the candidacies of legislators, gubernatorial

3

aspirants, and national politicians who fought for social reforms. As such, the urban lower class was instrumental in securing the hallmarks of the liberal political agenda including the rights of labor, child welfare regulations within the workplace, humane housing codes that appreciated the difference between an immediate necessity and the permenance of institutional degradation, sanitation ordinances that protected the health and dignity of those who, at best, were new and often silent before American officialdom.[2] Reform was underwritten through the electoral behavior of urban immigrants.

The same lower class political culture and consciousness, discernable when ethnic voting histories are examined, serve as evidence and testimony to a political involvement and social agenda which was preeminently progressive. Huthmacher questioned, therefore, the exclusivity of progressive reform being both dominated by and inspired by the middle class; or, in kind, whether Protestantism deserved the rather singular focus as the progressive movement's ethical and philosophical wellspring.[3] In fact, the archetype of the progressive reformer may have been society's underlings: namely, the urban immigrant who rapidly got the lay of the political landscape because progressive reform made immediate or practical sense. In other words, the progressive political agenda was defined by those, at least in part, who needed reform the most and to whom political rhetoric was an insufficient substitute for actual political performance.[4]

And yet, the great bulk of historical proof needed to sustain the Huthmacher thesis was only hypothesized by him, or at best, based upon Boston politics with a most circumspect treatment of the ethnic enclaves which characterized Massachusetts' life in the first quarter of the century. Despite Huthmacher's persuasive writings and even more intriguing questions regarding ethnic politics and political participation in an age of social and popular reform, few

researchers have undertaken the task of unearthing
constituencies of ethnic progressives. At best, "newer America
have been accorded a place within the urban progressive phalan
but usually as a supportive clique to Democratic or Republican
political machines. Progressivism, as such, has been interpreted as a
sweeping reform movement, extraordinarily diverse and
multifaceted, but beyond the ken of lower class people, who allegedly
had neither the time nor the inclination to deliberate upon the body
politic. Allegedly, progressivism filtered or trickled down to lower
class urbanites as far as the process of Americanization intended. We
have been led to believe that the quest for social order and political
integrity, therefore, spurred the immigrant on to respond to the call
of the progressive reformer and, more importantly, to adopt an
accommodating, orderly brand of citizenship.

Any self generated or intuitive political insight or social
wisdom, or sense of societal improvement imbued within the
immigrant, was unassumed, ignored, or believed to be American
inspired. Thus, progressivism's middle class and Anglo-Saxon
wellsprings, however actual or exclusive they in fact were, have
monopolized the tone and focus of twentieth century historical study.
Huthmacher's scholarship, notwithstanding, lower class ethnic
people remain unrecognized as progressive reformers, and this
aspect of their historical record remains neglected.[5]

This study examines the Jewish and, to a far lesser extent, the
Irish voting and social record of a small Massachusetts city that, it is
argued, illuminates ethnic prejudice and politics in an age of
progressive reform. Malden, Massachusetts lies about seven miles
north of Boston. From 1900-1932 the city contained the most solidly
voting Irish-Democratic constituency in all Massachusetts. Irish

Malden in the year of President William Howard Taft's visit, 1912

Malden Square about 1920

dominated Ward 2 was populated by nearly 10,000-15,000 individuals. Living in two and three tenement dwellings located between the Boston and Maine Railroad tracks and the rather prodigious manufacturing and industrial plants tucked throughout the ward, the Irish made their home amid the thick smokestacks that belched a dark odoriferous cloud announcing rubber was king. In addition, the local Irish work force labored in the tanneries, chemical plants, and a multitude of other industrial workplaces that gave Malden a decidedly blue collar ambience.

And yet the city was distinguished as the ancestral home of a proud, prosperous, but somewhat intellectually isolated Yankee population.[6] The late nineteenth century writer, Harriet H. Robinson, was a fifty year resident of the city to which she moved in 1857. At that time she noted the following about Malden. "A strange

Feeding the ducks at The Middlesex Fells Park, c. 1905

Girls in Pine Banks Park, 1907

place, but near Boston and we like it. It certainly costs less to live there and we enjoy it more." Robinson's recent biographer observed that the city possessed "beautiful woody heights and rocky glens" but the city began to lose many of its older families who moved to more exclusive, nearby towns such as Medford or Winchester.[7] Doubtless, the fact that Malden attracted diverse ethnic peoples who inhabited a frequently hodge podge assortment of dwellings led to the city's social decline. As one of its more renowned city father's noted, somewhat wistfully,

> Malden retains few of the features of the past. You miss the narrow lanes, the wide green fields, and the dark woods of your youthful days. You miss the fragrant wild rose and the sweet brier by the wayside. For you the mill-pond gleams no more, and the salt tides come no more among the edges and flags of

8

Harvell's Brook, where the blackbird built her nest. The rocky crest of Whyte's Mount seems not so near the clouds as in the days of your childhood; and the arethusa blooms and the cranberry ripens no more in Blanchard's meadows. The advancing tides of population have swept away the charms of the country side.[8]

As part of that human tide, the city became home to what would grow to be one of the largest concentrations of Jews north of Boston. Ward 7 and particularly the Suffolk Square section of the ward became the focal point of a politically active and socially concerned Jewish community. For example,over 200,000 Jews lived in Massachusetts by 1929 with about 70,000 living in Boston. While Boston possessed a Jewish population that numbered anywhere from fifty to eighty thousand from 1910-1930, Malden's Jewish population approached over 9,000 residents by 1921, and would swell to nearly 15,000 Jews through the 1940's. At its height, this represented a bit less than a quarter of the entire population of Malden.[9] In a number of ways, Malden's Jews epitomized many of those 2.7 million Jews who emigrated to the United States from Poland and Russia from 1900-1924. While the large eastern cities, New York in particular, witnessed prominent and now well documented Jewish community life, some three out of ten Jewish immigrants settled in smaller cities and towns.[10] Cities such as Malden typified the social milieu that small city Jewry probably experienced, particularly as they set about making their life and their livelihood at small scale entrepreneurship. First generation Jews in Malden, and countless others in similar cities and towns throughout the nation, were concerned with a social agenda and political questions that directly affected both their immediate lives and, even more, their dreams for themselves and their children.[11]

As such, Malden's pluralistic population, its metropolitan

The fruit and vegetable store, c. 1905

location, and its politically active citizenry make the study of small city Jewish existence ideal. In particular the following questions were considered: how did Jews and other ethnics vote and participate in an era of progressive reform? What political personalities brought ethnics together and/or kept them apart in the evolution of America's political culture? Do state or local political developments, evidenced in Malden's ethnic voting records, reflect national voting trends for the period? Finally, in what ways did Jewish and other ethnic constituencies contribute to what we understand as America's cultural pluralism?

In effect, this study explores the immigrant role in the 1900-1932 period, and how those "tides of population" helped define both reform and politics in the countless Malden's throughout the nation.

Chapter One

A Jew Must Be A Jew

Newcomers to Malden, c. 1904

Into the twentieth century, the core of Malden's identity as a community was the civic pride of its Protestant families, and their strong sense of a common past. Doubtless, this pride was reflected in their homes, and indeed the physical environment which they had tendered and cultivated. Large, gracious Victorian houses dotted the hilly West side of the city. They were constructed of stone, quarried nearby, or of wooden frame construction with tastefully painted clapboards, surrounded by large porches in an ideal suburban setting. Often, they contained a small carriage house affixed to the main living quarters that, by the early 1900's, was rapidly being converted to an automobile garage. Although the two or even three story structures sometimes contained fifteen to nearly twenty rooms, their lots of land tended to be compact, nicely shrubbed, and carefully attended. Inside the house, the furnishings of the large rooms reflected less concern for opulence or even comfort and more for the business of living. Whether compelled by social status or financial ease, the cold East winds of the Atlantic dictated that steam heat be an added "modern" convenience. Large, oftentimes noisy radiators pounded as forced steam clanked through the network pipes. And at no added expense, their proprietors boasted, hot water was plentiful and free especially during the long winter. In Malden, one's heating system belied one's social class.

And yet, to those who appreciated and understood "old" Malden, the grandeur and beauty of life was to be experienced in its almost bucolic countryside existence, whose quality and pace of life seemed never to change.

A clapboard and stone house in the West End of the city

Standing as pillars and monuments to the community's common heritage were the city's churches. Moving eastward as one would toward the direction of the sea, which was but a couple of miles from Malden's border, stood a large Methodist church that was as constantly in need of repairs as were its congregants in need of spare cash. The church was located in Malden's Linden neighborhood, home to Eliot Paul, born in Linden in 1891, one of the city's many authors and artists. His remembrances of his childhood, entitled *Linden On The Saugus Branch*, reflected upon the local church architecture because it symbolized both Malden's historical identity and her socio-political anxieties.[1]

> There were never any fine old houses, examples of Colonial or European architecture, and none of the new houses were remarkable for their proportion or lines. The churches or meeting houses, post-dated the period when blinds and white steeples made the house of God in New England villages an expression of dignity or beauty. Linden's churches were aesthetic monstrosities, badly designed, jerry-built, and inexpertly painted.[2]

Paul recognized quite perceptively that his hilly section of the city possessed little in the way of grand Victorian homes; nonetheless, the small houses and their self-sufficient occupants existed in overall contentment, albeit estrangement, from the city's more affluent Protestant neighbors living in other sections of the city far from Linden.

The more influential and prestigious Congregational Church of Linden was noted for its loud, clanging bell that was housed in a square wooden tower. Standing smack in the center of its basement, used as a Sunday school room, was a huge, often cantankerous furnace, "that fed smoke, powdered ashes and hot air into the registers of the main auditorium upstairs." Paul recalled that "the older members of the congregation, in point of membership, had pews near the register, which were spotted along the aisles."[3] Paul recalled: "The Linden men and women liked to think of themselves as slightly above average Americans, not too smart, and certainly not stupid or provincial." It was this inconspicuous aspect of Linden's

A small house on Salem Street, c. 1910

identity that echoed in the minds of its citizenry: "No Linden pioneers had a conspicuous part in building up our nation. And if any nineteenth or twentieth century residents set the planet afire, in any field or endeavor, I have not been informed of the fact." In fact, Linden's geography murmured obscurity, too. "It was neither backwoods, seashore, country, city or town, but only a detached precinct of the outermost ward of the suburban city of Malden, eight or nine miles distant from Boston, as the crow flies." "Linden was hilly, rural, isolated politically from the larger city, and considered a poor relation to their cross town fellow Protestants."[4]

Nonetheless, Linden was loved and indelibly etched in the hearts of its residents. In this neighborhood and, clearly, in all the neighborhoods of 19th century Malden, had existed a stability of community life in which "change grew imperceptibly like trees, maintaining the community's form and shape on a slowly expanding scale . . . Men who did not like to work for wages had

A stable in the Maplewood section of Malden, c. 1895

small businesses of their own."⁵ There was a confidence in the seasons and a certainty to life that, unsurprisingly, waned and nearly dissipated as the city grew in population, wealth, and ethnic diversity.

> Great fortunes had been made. The names of J. Pierpont Morgan, John D. Rockefeller, and John Jacob Astor were bandied about in the newspapers and magazines, and there were a few Massachusetts millionaires not well known locally. The trusts were talked of as a bugaboo, but Linden men were mostly conservative, and believed that the smart, successful men knew what they were doing and that the country was safe in their hands.⁶

It was clear, at least to Eliot Paul, what brought on those social changes that obliterated Linden's self-sufficiency and satisfaction

17

with the *status quo*. It was ambition. Reflectively, Paul mused on Linden's ambitious paperboy: "He never was late. He never made mistakes. He saved the pennies he earned . . . He was not very smart in school, but he was tenacious, and never missed a grade!" Characteristically, Paul concluded, "I was then and always since then have been a little in awe of men, young or old, who were hustlers and whose career was clear to them and could be built step by step, according to a plan."[7]

And the more that Malden changed in terms of its diverse population, politics, technological developments, and other aspects of twentieth century existence, Linden was forced to change, too. Progress brought electrification for a street railway company, and Linden's first fire station; people, changed too, with the Irish establishing a small parish within Linden. Beyond the marshes, in nearby Revere, large numbers of Italians were settling, disturbing the tranquility of Linden life, or so it seemed to Linden people.[8]

Linden kids, c. 1910

It was alleged, by property owners in Linden, that the presence of Italians lowered property values within the community. Paul noted that "the Linden women did not relish the strong smell of garlic on the trolley cars." And even more annoying was the fact that the Italians purchased and refurbished ramshackle buildings or otherwise dilapidated wrecks. These "Italian homesteaders" proceeded to spend all day Sunday "in full view of the Linden churchgoers, [and] worked with old boards, tar paper, second hand window frames and doors, hammer and nails, pick and shovel, building and gardening from dawn until dark."[9]

But it was the influx of Jews that most upset the people of Linden, and Eliot Paul's memories were riveted on this reality.

> No Jew ever lived in Linden ... Quite early in the century, when surrounding communities were receiving a steady influx of Jews, the Linden Protestants and the more prosperous Catholics who owned their homes banded together into what was called the 'Linden Improvement Association.' No one, in my hearing, questioned its propriety or called it Un-American.
> .. The purpose of the Linden Improvement Association was to protect real estate values in Linden, which meant a thoroughgoing understanding between all property owners that neither houses or lots would ever be sold to Jews. It was purely a business proposition. Wherever the Jews crowded in, as they had already in Chelsea and Faulkner [Ward 7, the Suffolk Square area], property values went down, and the Jewish children swarmed into the schools, Jewish adults bought up all the small and large businesses, and Gentiles had either to become a minority without influence or pull up stakes and move.[10]

Paul's memoirs of Linden, published in 1947, boasted that "the men

I liked most, the most liberal and jolly and tolerant and companionable, were charter members of the Improvement Association. They included my Uncle Reuben, Great Uncle Lije, my brother Charles, practically all the Protestant deacons, small business men, and Protestants who worked in Boston."[11]

Anti-Semitism in Linden was a lingering theme of Paul's earliest writings. A 1924 novel *Impromptu*, one of his first, was set in the town of "Glendale."

> A few years before nineteen seven, the Glendale Improvement Association had been organized. Faulkner, a station but two from Glendale on the Saugus branch, began to be overrun with Jews. Ugly three deckers of the cheapest construction had been erected within sight of the railroad tracks and the Glendale commuters could see each evening fat Jewish mothers resting their flopping breasts on the window sills and could hear shrill children swarming the back streets. All the available houses in Faulkner were purchased by Jews and were rented by Jews, heaven knows how many packed into a room! . . . so the Glendale Improvement Association had organized. All vacant lots and empty houses were purchased, and it was understood that foreigners, especially Jews, were to be excluded in future from the town.[12]

Italians, Jews and the Irish, too, threatened Linden and all of Malden. After all, was not ambition the sin of the Jews? And yet the people of Linden felt no comfort with poverty as a sign of nobility or sinlessness! Linden's people sensed that their lives were changing. Paul recognized it in his own family, as his brother Charles' dreams of success were contrasted to his own uncharted and chaotic sense of the future.

No one in Linden doubted, however, that the local Jews were

either indecisive or hesitant about the future. Indeed, to the people of Linden, the local Jews personified those people who felt comfort in a societal change that could only adversely affect the natives of old Malden. Eliot Paul's recollections of anti-Semitism in Linden provide but a hint of that "institutional" prejudice encountered by Malden's Jews and other ethnics as they made a new life in what was an old city.

Opportune ethnics made Linden shutter, for the "ambitious" Jews sought a share of America's promise, specifically "the dream closest to each immigrant's heart . . . to own his home and a plot of ground in free America."[13]

The overwhelming majority of Jews in Malden lived nearby in Ward 7, the Suffolk Square area. At the turn of the new century, Malden's earliest Jews pioneered as tailors or peddlers or junkmen, who found their economic opportunities among the Irish of Ward 2 and, somewhat ironically, even in Linden. Frequently, as in Linden, the local tailor and the itinerant junkman were quite popular and well liked. They, of course, did not live in Linden but they traded and worked within the community, and were hardly reluctant to talk about their Jewishness.

> Moe made and pressed the suits, honestly, gaily and in a citizen-like manner. Moe had taken out his first [citizenship] papers. Ben had not, although he intended to some time, and never got around to it until his son came home from Dartmouth College in time for the First World War.[14]

In Ward 2, south of Linden, a small number of Jews worked in the Irish community as craftsmen, shopkeepers, and

Husbands and wives...

...in their new city

tradesmen. In 1907, some thirty-five Jewish men met for worship among themselves, finding it too difficult to walk across the city to the Orthodox synagogues in Ward 7. Ward 2's or Edgeworth's Orthodox Jews initially hoped to establish a synagogue of their own, but the size of Edgeworth's Jewish population never amounted to more than a *minyan,* or the necessary ten men for worship.[15] The Edgeworth Hebrew Association existed until about 1910. Nonetheless, the centrality of Suffolk Square and its Jewish religious life negated any need for a Jewish satellite congregation in Edgeworth.[16]

Suffolk Square was the center of Ward 7, located at a small intersection of three winding thoroughfares used by horses and

From 1920 to almost 1960, Suffolk Square...

buggies and, later, the electrified trolleys of the Boston Elevated System.

Whatever the means of transportation to and from the Square, the purpose for going there remained very much the same for decades. Numerous Jewish food stores existed in one convenient location. Specialty stores contained barrels of pickles in assorted concoctions of spices or garlic. The large window of a Jewish fishmarket displayed their fish on a bed of ice, fish eyes fascinating the children who gazed at them. There, at the corner fishmarket was also the local gathering spot for the old and young or just those looking for conversation.

In many respects, kibitzing was a cross between recreation and avocation. Particular establishments boasted that their large blocks of cream cheese or farmer's cheese or stacks of smoked fishes were without equal in greater Boston. Jewish bakeries were known for

...remained nearly unchanged

their breads and bulkie rolls; others were held in esteem for their pastries or selection of sugar cookies. Restaurants offered the home cooked delicacies of *kugels*, *tsimas*, *flanken* or beef dishes, assorted roasted chicken and chicken soups, and desserts that reflected an extraordinary Eastern European ambience upon the small makeshift Square.

The ancestral delicacies of Russian Jewry versus those of Lithuanian Jewry were debated and boasted of in a good natured rivalry. Suffolk Square grocers stocked the packaged and canned noodles, gefilte fish, and countless other food stuffs. Dry goods stores, fruit stores, drugstores, candy stores, variety stores, luncheonettes, a Jewish cooperative bank, and about a half dozen kosher butcher shops displayed their goods and services with an unabashed pride and naturalness. Undoubtedly, the strong religious nature of Malden's Jews was reflected in the multitude of kosher butcher shops which carried on a brisk and busy trade; order boys pushing large, square-shaped carts could be seen throughout the area, dropping off the wrapped bundles of meat often too heavy for a shopper to carry. In butcher store windows, one observed a clothesline of chickens hanging by their wings, with their feathers unplucked, amid trays of sliced or cut meats, other trays of chopped liver, cartons of eggs piled high, weighing scales atop meat chests and densely packed show cases, and the lingering smell of the daily cleansed butcher's block. Their heads covered by a kerchief, a *yamaka*, or a hat, Yiddish speaking men conversed with their neighbors and their customers.

At no time were the stores more busy than Thursday afternoons or at the latest, by early Friday morning, as the citizenry prepared for the Sabbath. No later than two o'clock on Friday afternoon, the butcher shops closed. The bakeries bustled with the sale of *challahs* or desserts such as jelly rolls. And the nearby Y-D bottling plant did a land-office business in the bottled beverages of ginger ale, cream soda, or other fruit colored "tonics" thought essential for the evening meal. The smells of foods being prepared wafted throughout the tenements that surrounded Suffolk Square. And the bustle of shoppers and street traffic seemed to be in constant motion, with bundle-laden men or women interrupting the flow of traffic as they stopped to say hello, or ask about a *landslayt* or fellow towns person not recently seen.

Six synagogues served the Jews of Ward 7. Five were Orthodox congregations and one was more Conservative in tone. Each held both morning and afternoon *minyans*; each possessed a men's and women's auxiliary served by elected officers who oversaw the financial responsibility of each congregation, provided relief for the local poor, provided for proper burials of the destitute, and generally served as a religious body whose very existence testified that an observantly practiced Judaism remained the essence of a still new American existence. Jewish teachings reiterated the need for Jews "to be Jews", regardless of geography, and this had great meaning to the first generation American.

Frequently, wealthy congregants supplied the necessary funds for construction or repairs of their synagogues. As such, their religious buildings were neat and orderly, simple in design, with bench like seats for all. During the High Holiday period of each year of *Rosh Hashanah* and *Yom Kippur*, the synagogues were jammed with people. The nearby streets became a maze of people. Overflow crowds and mingling congregants gathered in the streets before, during, and after the services. Indeed, the streets were laden with Jewish children and young people socializing or taking a few moments to catch a breath of air from the non-stop Yom Kippur religious services. Even non-observant Jews were to be found, properly dressed, outside the synagogues. Respect for those who worshipped demanded that non-believers make, at the least, an appearance; those who demeaned the High Holidays flirted with apostacy, and what was more, demeaned the Jewish people in the eyes of the Gentiles.

For Jews, as well as Gentiles, and all who actually remember Malden's Jewish quarter, the area evoked vivid and heartfelt memories of that lively place. Indeed, the smells, sounds, and sights of Suffolk Square remain a part of the collective memory of the city and to all those who recall its past.[17]

Jewish children often were seen in the Square, trailing their parents or mingling with their peers, and their memories of the Square have provided the stories and memories, subsequently, for their own children of Jewish life there.

And yet it would be incorrect to believe that Suffolk Square was anything but the *pulse* of Jewish life in Malden. Clearly, it was on the pavements and in the apartments of the many side streets and courts that surrounded the Square which was the heart of Malden Jewry. In tenements, duplexes, three-deckers, two-families, and within the boarding houses of Ward 7, Jewish family life was re-rooted from the villages and towns of Eastern Europe. Somewhat nervously, a local newspaper reported that as early as 1904 almost an entire precinct from two precincts of Ward 7, had grown to be "almost all Jews!"[18]

By referring to the poll books of Malden, one can chart Jewish population movements throughout the entire ward, documenting the ward's transformation from rural farmland to an ethnic ghetto.[19] In 1900, this had been a predominantly Protestant, lower middle class ward with about ten percent of its population identifiable as Irish working people and, at best, three percent Jewish residents. The poll books supply data regarding the names, addresses, occupations, and age of its residents. Using Suffolk Square as a focal point, one can make relatively accurate assessments regarding ethnicity based on surname, address and occupation of the occupants. Similarly, a discernable pattern existed in Ward 2, too, and using surnames and residences accounts for the following assessments of the Irish presence and history within that ward.

Besides surname and occupation, the age of the residents becomes important in understanding the Jewish presence within Ward 7. Jewish heads of households invariably reported their ages as ranging from the mid-thirties to late forties from 1900 right through the 1920's. By 1928 with nearly seventy-five percent of the Ward identifiable as Jewish, this age trend abated, and a more diverse and varied population emerged. The fact remains, however, that Jewish emigration to Malden involved young through middle aged parents with many grammar school-aged children. Heads of households worked as tailors, meat cutters, peddlers, haulers and dispensers of provisions, pressers and packers to the garment industry, cigar makers, and associated manufacturers. By 1912, well over fifty percent of Ward 7's residents were Jewish and barely twenty percent can be identified by surname or occupation as Protestant. By 1928, the Protestant population of the ward became eclipsed and was absent from the polling records. Only particular bordering streets adjacent to nearby wards possessed a population identifiable with the Irish or an emerging Italian constituency.

Within the Jewish community, however, the poll books reveal a certain pronounced economic condition. There existed a core of Jewish shopkeepers, a tiny number of professionals, and a broad category of service people (from tailors to plumbers). There was an apparent evolution of job consciousness or job upgrading that developed as the number of peddlers dwindled; those who called themselves salesmen or merchants increased dramatically handling sundry goods including furniture, housewares, hats and caps, and other dry goods. Insurance salesmen proliferated. Specialized crafts boomed, especially plasterers, tinsmiths, upholsterers, masons, plumbers, and butchers. The poll books provide an indispensable view of the Jewish occupational diversity and direction within the ward.

The local press noted the changes brought on by Malden's Jewish residents. Once familiar landmarks soon became identified with the Jews. For example, the press reported that the Faulkner Methodist Church had been purchased for use as Malden's first permanent synagogue.[20] On the eve of its first day of use as a synagogue, one of its Jewish congregants climbed to the top of its spire to remove its crucifix, but with nothing else to place in its stead. The dedication of this new Congregation Beth Israel was celebrated as an example of the city's vigorous and expanding Jewish communal activities.[21]

Second only to the synagogue was a belief in the religious education for children, and by 1910 a comprehensive religious school had been constructed in the ward.[22] Local charity and philanthropy underwrote the construction of "the House of Solomon Talmud Torah." The school was predicated on the necessity of Jewish education as a community responsibility, and fees were subject to the ability of a student's family to pay. Fundraising for educational and charitable needs was undertaken by diverse Jewish organizations including the Hebrew Ladies Aid Association, Young Men's Hebrew Association, and the Hebrew Charitable Association. By 1915 the building housed the Young Men's Hebrew Association, for example, a central meeting place for lectures, vocals, and recitations; in addition, a Junior Zionist Literary Club met there for parties and discusssions. In 1915, Jewish debating societies, at the Y.M.H.A. and at Beth Israel Synagogue, brought religious and civic questions before the community, including the call for a worldwide gathering to discuss Jewish problems. Also, in 1915, the topic of "National Preparedness of the United States for War" was debated.[23] According to the founders of the Y.M.H.A., its purpose for existing was for "conducting its affairs along the lines of educational, civic, and religious advantages for the Jewish people."[24] This was a vibrant

A young Jewish family in Malden, c. 1910

cultural organization that was widely recognized for its theatre and dramatics.

The Jews of Malden freely and proudly exhibited their ethnic and religious identity. Utilizing the local press, they made the larger Malden community aware of their *Chanukah* parties as well as their political and social concerns. They marched in the streets of Malden to express their indignation regarding injustices to fellow Jews in Poland and Russia, and they protested regarding injustices to themselves in Malden. With their votes as well as their feet, Malden Jewry possessed the inclination to participate in political and philosophical questions and debates of the day, and frequently, they ventured into arguments that were beyond their immediate lives or economic circumstances.

While they struggled to adjust to life in America, they continued to respect a kind of religious obligation to give to those in financial need and to demonstrate their solidarity with Jews and non-Jews seeking social justice. Neither their newness to America nor the cultural adjustment inevitable to their condition excused the Orthodox Jew to be idle or passive in his civic duties. An analysis of Jewish voting in Malden must recognize this fact as well as appreciate those specific local conditions that contributed to shaping their political legacy.

Clearly, financial goals and aspirations influenced their political philosophy, too. Jewish economic advancement was predicated upon the promise of America, the *Golden Door*, and the actualization of real opportunity was the litmus test of their hopes. The Jews of Malden were filled with a belief in themselves as individuals, and despite often feeling beleaguered, they found joy in their blossoming community, this small city in America.

Eagerly, they sought to demonstrate that their Jewishness would contribute towards and enhance America's commitment to the needs of an aspiring humanity and a philosophy of unbridled opportunity. As a recent writer has correctly observed, the Jews were impressed with the idea that the *goyim* or Gentiles of America were different.[25] In the old world, the Gentiles negated the humanity of the Jew, ascribing near mythical and thoroughly prejudicial qualities to them so as to lower and debase Jewish humanity. But in America, and especially during the Progressive period, Jews were impressed with progressive Americans who preached civic resonsibility, economic opportunity, and tolerance. Why should the racist musings of Malden's Eliot Paul, who was an admitted misfit, make the Jews think negatively about their new city or their new neighbors?

Chapter Two

Ethnic Coalitions, Real and Imagined

A political moment in the life of the city, c. 1910

In America, and specifically in Malden, the contradictions of America's promise were far from invisible. There was a peculiar American *shtik*, translated as a local or Gentile ambivalence, regarding the Jewish presence, that made Jews recognize essential truths about their citizenship in Malden. Neither Democrats nor Republicans sought to ally Jewish voters to their party's banner. State and local politicians neither volunteered political favors to the local Jews, nor did the Jews seek out political favors, jobs, or other indulgences associated with the fruits of political association. Indeed, Jewish voting was frequently unpredictable; and it was generally shunned. The Jewish vote exhibited a high degree of political discernment, and was oblivious to the need for political compromises or the expectation of political rewards.

Through the first three decades of the twentieth century the East European Jews that settled in the United States tended to identify with the Republican Party, at least those Jews outside of New York and probably other Democratic strongholds where the party apparatus was responsive to the political and economic aspirations of predominantly lower class constituents.[1] As we shall see, Malden's Jews were attracted to Massachusetts' Republican ideology on behalf of expanded economic opportunities for individuals who sought America's promise through the marketplace, while at the same time, the Republican inspired government boasted a steady record of progressive legislation. Doubtless, Republican advancement on behalf of both economic opportunity and social justice appealed to the religious sentiments of the overwhelmingly Orthodox Jews of Malden, who strove for ethical ideals in the affairs of men, but were also quite impressed by the rhetoric of a free market economy and the demonstrative economic accomplishments of Malden's many industries and firms.

In part, even Jewish economic life in the city was remarkably isolated from both the city's blue- and white-collar work forces, established industries, and even its retail economy. Malden was a divided city, characterized by an assortment of ethnic ghettoes, or, more graphically, a number of mini-states.[2] As we shall see, the Jewish quarter and the Jewish presence in Malden was viewed with ambiguity by the city's Yankee-Republicans and the Irish-Democrats for reasons peculiar to each group.

In the election of 1912, Teddy Roosevelt's Progressive Party polled 50.8% of Ward 7's vote to some 27.5% for Woodrow Wilson, while incumbent President Taft received 21.7% of the total vote.[3] Wilson's showing was the ward's highest voting percentage for a Democratic presidential candidate up until that election, and may have been related to the fact that Wilson was endorsed by the prestigious *The Jewish Advocate*.[4] Nonetheless, in Wilson's reelection contest of 1916, he failed to carry the ward, although by under 3% of the vote. In the gubernatorial contest of 1912, Malden Jews continued to support the candidacy of Eugene Foss, in that election running as the Democratic standard-bearer. In 1913, Foss ran as a Progressive, third party candidate and received 33.2% of the vote. The Republican gubernatorial candidate, Charles Bird, experienced an election defeat probably because of Foss' presence in the campaign.

In the meantime, one of the Commonwealth's most prominent and electorally successful Democrats, David I. Walsh, won the governorship in 1913 but had a dismal record among Malden Jewry. In that election, Walsh received 17.3% of Ward 7's vote. Governor Walsh, Massachusetts' first Irish Catholic governor, received 35.4% of the ward's vote in what would prove to be a successful reelection bid in 1914 against Samuel McCall who received some 64% of the Ward 7 vote. In Walsh's defeat for a third term in 1915, McCall polled a strong 60% of Ward 7's vote to Walsh's 37%.[5] In fact, Walsh did less well among Malden Jewry than almost anywhere among Massachusetts' ethnic enclaves.

Republicans and Democrats found Malden Jewry somewhat less than consistent in their voting allegiance. In fact, Ward 7 rejected political leadership that was viewed as arrogant, insensitive to the aspirations of lower class and especially ethnic peoples. The Jewish vote possessed a sense of social conscience that proved far more electorally consistent than the often silent and vacuous brand of Progressivism practiced by both parties in the Bay State. In fact, the Walsh years are illustrative of certain electoral trends that help demystify the first generation Jewish vote.

Walsh's failure to garner a favorable vote of Ward 7 was predicated, at least in part, on the Democratic Party's inability to convince Jewish voters that they mattered. The Irish versus Yankee battles which typified Walsh's early elections negatively influenced Jewish voters. To the first generation Jewish voters, the Irish victory at the polls was neither progressive in political intent or in the building of a social order predicated on ethnic rapproachment. To this first generation of Jewish voters, the Irish prevailed at the polls because of their unrelenting energies and incessant demand for recognition. In and of itself, however noble the Irish stirring was, Irish politicians failed to convince Ward 7 that Democratic politics were anything but parochial power struggles. In Massachusetts, Democratic politicians sought political respectability at the expense of a focused, political ideology.

For example, Walsh's inaugural address of 1914 before the Massachusetts legislature was a measured and well reasoned assessment of the Commonwealth's needs.[6] His call for biennial gubernatorial elections, for example, was to eliminate the continual electioneering for the state's top offices and, instead, concentrate on the actual implementation of a governor's program. Yet aside from the traditional recitations regarding the operation of the state, Walsh's message was in fact a call for ethnic peace in the Commonwealth. Quoting from President Lincoln's Second Inaugural Address of March 4, 1865 after four years of Civil War, Walsh reached out to those who viewed his victory as onerous or as a "revolution."

> With malice toward none
> with charity for all;
> with firmness in the right,
> as God gives us the right,
> let us strive on to finish
> the work we are in.[7]

But to Massachusetts Yankees, Walsh was still very much an Irish-Democratic governor, Massachusetts' first, and was attacked almost instantly as a big government man, a spender, and a featherbedder of public payrolls.

There was something unconvincing and hollow about Walsh. At least in his gubernatorial career, Walsh's political identity was molded by a cautious deportment and an affinity to middle class sensitivities. If he aspired to be a political insurgent or the representative of the Massachusetts dispossessed, he did not convince Malden's Jews of this intention. In fact, Walsh was unsure of who he was. His political campaigns, at least for governor, never adequately joined the diverse lower class peoples and interests that a social crusader or such a clear representative of Massachusetts' ethnics required. Tragically, Walsh sought middle class approval from Yankee and certain "lace curtain" Irish quarters, and missed the unique opportunity of establishing broader ethnic and social class appeal around himself and the Democratic Party.[8]

In fact, first generation Jews found little of a personal nature to differentiate between candidates such as McCall and Walsh. McCall's reputation as an "independent" legislator, undeserved by a rather stand-pat performance as a Congressman, was to some, nonetheless, a symbol of integrity.

He was also known as an author and essayist. After his political career, in 1924, McCall authored a volume entitled *Patriotism of the American Jew*. With a forward written by the president of Harvard University, Charles W. Eliot, McCall was praised for his scholarship and public commitment to religious tolerance. McCall wrote about Jewish service to mankind and America. The former governor urged his readers to reject racism and prejudice against Jews, sentiments that gained favor as a result of the popularity of the anti-Semitic tract, *The Protocols of the Elders of Zion*, and a variety of anti-immigrant legislation and nativist attitudes.[9] In a philosophical and highly emotional passage, McCall stated his earnest hope for America.

> If there is one particular in which the course of the American Commonwealth is clear, it is that it should strive to incorporate into one harmonious whole the various races of which it is

composed and that it should not tolerate the creation of a variety of social and political ghettos which shall enclose the different race groups. To do that would be to contrive against our own greatness and permanence as a state.[10]

Undoubtedly, McCall was representative of that Yankee libertarian strain whose message was unabashedly moral and dogmatic. As such, there was a rich blend of both politics and morality which appealed to first generation Jews. The humanity of political questions and the *menshlikayt* or true humanness of its spokesman was revered in Jewish thought. In truth, McCall's tract possessed an extraordinary element of *noblesse oblige*. He was patronizing and perhaps even insensitive to the strengths of American pluralism. But first generation Jews were only too painfully aware of their delicate condition: they were immigrants in a promising yet strange land, believing in the *Golden Door* of America's opportunities, and appreciative of praise, however self-serving the praise may have been. The courteous and wealthy Yankee was honored for his *menshlikayt*; his condescension was considered but an affectation.

Any Democratic Party candidate would have been viewed somewhat less auspiciously than the prosperous Republican businessman-politician who preached the sacredness of economic opportunity for those willing to work and for social and political liberalism as an American ideology. Malden Jews voted for McCall and other Republicans fashioned on his model.

David Walsh's two terms as governor were remarkable in that an Irish Catholic from a minority political party could win Yankee Massachusetts. In Malden, most successful Irish-Catholic political candidates operated from the Republican Party. Walsh's political successes demonstrated the potential of Irish solidarity. In actuality, the Democratic Party's challenge of Massachusetts' Yankee hegemony could occur only with a united Irish core. Yet in Malden,

Walsh experienced the second great weakness of Irish-Democratic politics. The quest for Irish solidarity had obscured the necessity of a still broader based political alliance. With Walsh's victory, the process of courting potential Democratic converts gave way to the great reality of elective office: patronage. The absolute hunger of the Democratic Party for patronage, especially on the state level, forced Walsh first, to select personnel, then, unendingly to defend his political appointees and, finally, to explain an ever burgeoning state budget.Republican politicians hounded the Democrats regarding patronage and fiscal waste, often deflecting more serious consideration from Walsh's substantive reform programs. For example, Walsh's advocacy for biennial elections went unheeded, and expansion of the workman's compensation act, consolidation and modernizing of state government, and the assembling of a constitutional convention were rejected out of hand. Democrat-inspired reform became mired in an unending struggle; the more Walsh shouted for political reform, the more he was criticized for economic waste, featherbedding, and overall incompetence.

Walsh's governorship suffered, then, on two counts, both of which retarded his and other Irish appeals to individuals and groups such as Malden Jewry. Irish solidarity was crucial to his election, but in itself limited as a political accomplishment for his party's future successes. In addition, Walsh could not establish a political agenda or dictate the necessary initiative that concentrated upon progressive politics; instead, his forward looking policies were deflected from debate in place of repeated and defensive explanations over each political act and every "partisan" appointment. In a word, Walsh's election became the *raison d'etre* of his administration. Only when Walsh shifted his political base away from Beacon Hill to Capitol Hill did he expand both his constituency and articulate an individualized, unambigious political identity. The problems that Walsh encountered as an Irish officeholder were integral to the political problems of coalition building, especially when viewed from small American cities and towns. Walsh and others like him had difficulty communicating that his political problems grew out of prejudice rather than a poor political performance.

That America might be "as a city upon a hill" was extraordinarily pertinent and similar to a far more ancient philosophical imperative: a Jew must be a Jew. In other words, the small city Jew believed that the promise of life in America could only be realized by the maintenance of an ethical and personal sense of Jewish identity, the all important religious steadfastness, and their hope that America's reputation for political liberty would permit an almost suffocating Jewish activism to emerge. Life in Malden, though *shtetl*-like in many ways, offered seemingly boundless opportunities for the new immigrants. In their dreams if not by their immediate reality, the Jews were impressed by life there, inland between the Mystic River and the Atlantic Ocean. A Jewish joke at the time was that life in America was so orderly and estimable that, evidenced by reports in the daily newspapers, people even died in alphabetical order!

Malden Jewry was, doubtless, gratified that the most prominent members of Malden's population welcomed them. The Deliberative Society, Malden's most prestigious debating society and issues forum, often addressed questions relating to increased Jewish immigration within the United States or to the inhumane treatment of Jews in Czarist Russia. In the early years of the new century, Malden's Protestant majority reaffirmed the historical premise that America should serve as a refuge for those in need and that Jews should be saved from persecution, be allowed entry to the United States, and be permitted to take up their lives as citizens and residents of communities such as Malden.[11]

Indeed,the local Methodist Church invited Malden's earliest rabbi, Ber Boruchoff to address its church members so as to explain Judaism to the congregation as well as to welcome Jewry to Malden. The elder rabbi, who was the author of numerous religious articles and commentaries in both Hebrew and Aramaic, declined to address the group, but only because of his halting command of English. He sent his son in his place and his younger daughters accompanied his son. Many years afterwards, his daughter reflected, that many of her high school classmates appeared to look upon her and other Jews at the time with almost a degree of deference and respect. They felt fortunate to have such a noteworthy people in their midst.[12] Indeed, Rabbi Boruchoff was a most important religious and secular leader. Frequent visitors to his study included many well known Massachusetts dignitaries, including Henry Cabot Lodge and the Malden governor, Alvin Fuller.[13]

The son of Rabbi Ber Boruchoff was Raphael Boruchoff who, like his father and most other prominent Jews in Malden, was a lifelong Republican. In fact, he also was one of Malden's first Jewish elected officials, having been elected in 1920 to the city council from Ward 7. He was a vigorous exponent of Jewish life and Jewish political activism within the city and, indeed, throughout political reform circles. As the years went by, he was recognized as an important, influential barometer of political sentiment in Massachusetts. In 1933, he was elected the President of the civic reform organization, the Middlesex Civic League. In addition, Boruchoff served on numerous Republican Party platform committees where he, undoubtedly, doubled both as a representative of ethnic tokenism as well as an expression of the party's efforts of encouraging a more comprehensive ethnic constituency to the Republican fold.[14] As the son of the city's first rabbi and as a practicing attorney in the community, Raphael Boruchoff possessed a great deal of stature and respect among Malden Jewry. The fact that he was well over six feet tall reinforced the idea that his was a presence with which to reckon. This son of the rabbi served as the representative voice of the Jewish community. Versed in the Jewish tradition but trained in the law, Boruchoff possessed an immense social compassion. All who knew him, heard him speak, or worked in the many social and political causes in which he incessantly participated, marvelled at his energy, intellectual integrity, but most of all, his commitment to Jewish-American rights. The Jew, he believed, had much to teach America; Jewish ethics and the quest for legal equity shared a sense of universal compassion that, he thought, had a home in the Republican Party.

Chapter Three

"To Inherit the Earth"

Irish workmen taking a geological sample, c. 1895

Geographically, Malden's Irish were isolated from their Jewish neighbors in a most immediate way. Edgeworth lay amid Malden's factories and industrial furnaces. Huge brick and clapboard edifices included rubber works, soap factories, chemical companies, and the noxious smelling tanneries puffed grey and sooty smoke into the air that mingled with the winds coming off the ocean. In two and sometimes three working shifts per day, except for Sunday, Malden's rubber boots, boatshoes, and sneakers were the financial lifeblood to generations of Irish workers. And Edgeworth was home to a vast array of industries that found working space on the numerous single level, garages and warehouses that bounded the railroad.

Here, Malden's manufacturers moved for space to produce everything from horse harnesses to rubber tires so as to economically compete and reap the fortunes of America's industrial miracle. Products such as paint, varnishes, and brushes competed for a share of an increasingly national market, as did local soaps, medicines, and assorted parts for the automobile industry.[1] When the vicissitude of the economy brought an end to a particular industry, Malden's work space never lingered unused for long.

Entrepreneurs hoping to produce or refine a product, made Malden's warehouses the site of perpetual laboratories of invention. Literally, hundreds of small firms sprouted up throughout Ward 2, interspersing themselves between the criss-crossing railroad tracks.

And a number of influential nationally recognized firms originated and prospered in Edgeworth, most notably the Boston Rubber Shoe Company and its successor, the Converse Rubber Shoe Company. The Converse firm was a worldwide supplier for its wares, as was the Potter Drug and Chemical Corporation, whose soaps and acne preparations were advertised regularly in almost every New England newspaper. In fact, Cuticura soaps and skin creams became national standards and trade names in their own right. Spinning and dyeing companies, tanneries and machine tool firms, carriage, harness and saddle makers were particularly important to the local economy, and the periodic demise of such skilled crafts humbled Malden just as the antiquated shoe firms ended the prosperity of Lynn or nearby Brockton.

But most of all, Edgeworth was home to Malden's Irish, with Catholic worship dating from as early as 1822 in Edgeworth Chapel.[2]

In Malden rubber was king

The meandering Mystic River cut Edgeworth off from Catholic Charlestown, isolating its Irish population as Malden's Catholic enclave through the better part of the nineteenth and into the twentieth century. Always a densely populated neighborhood of two story clapboard houses, the number of streets increased and multiplied till the neighborhood could grow no more. Bordered on the east by the railroad right of way, Edgeworth was bounded on the west by the Fellsway, one of Massachusetts' most beautiful conservation areas containing woodlands, streams, walking paths, and a series of inland lakes used as emergency reservoirs. In fact, Fellsmere Pond cut Edgeworth off from growth to the north, besides the fact that here were developed prime suburban real estate lots for an influential neighborhood of Victorian estates, terraced on hilly, windy roads offering the most scenic land and skyscape north of Boston. Fellsmere Pond and Park were among the delights of Malden's suburban Yankee residents and a refuge for the city's most distinguished citizens.

Across town, as the crow flies, was Ward 7, until the late nineteenth century a virgin area but the site of the very spacious, seemingly boundless and beautiful Holy Cross Cemetery.

In Edgeworth, the Irish lived amid the factories, their exclusive workplaces. Life in Edgeworth possessed many of those qualities associated with the Irish neighborhoods of Boston, New York, or Philadelphia. Family life was an indispensible force in the stability of the neighborhood. In fact, after examination of over thirty years of police records, for example, Edgeworth was extraordinarily peaceful and internally disciplined. Juvenile delinquency was nearly nonexistent. Apparently, neighbors' quarrels rarely escalated into violence; rowdyism and brawling were equally rare. Edgeworth was quiet and humble and dignified. The citizenry possessed an immense pride in itself and its Irish heritage. Each year a special neighborhood party took place in which the oldest residents of Edgeworth paraded

and were the object of the community celebration.[3] The Irish
contribution to Edgeworth's industry was a source of pride, too:
they fired those huge furnaces and labored by workbenches that
brought the city both prosperity and economic recognition.

A bride and her brother, c. 1940

The Church of the Immaculate Conception was originally located between Malden and neighboring Medford. In 1866, the church served the populations of Stoneham, South Reading (Wakefield), part of Everett, as well as Malden and Medford. But Malden's Catholic population exploded between 1865 and 1905 due in great part to the proliferation of the city's industries and economic prominence.

Father Richard Neagle, Chancellor of the Boston Archdiocese, instructed Father Thomas H. Shahan, then rector of nearby Arlington, to erect a church more accessible and exclusive to the needs of Malden's Catholics. On May 5, 1901, Father Shahan officiated at the completion of a "large and beautiful church of the Sacred Heart, in the Romanesque style, which was dedicated by the Archbishop." On March 15, 1902, a separate parish was created for the Catholics on Malden's east side. By 1923, the number of Italian Catholics numbered nearly one thousand. Located on Pearl Street and originally a Protestant church, now named St. Peter's Chapel, it served Italians through Italian-speaking priests.[4]

Religious life was central to the identity of Edgeworth. As early as 1852, Edgeworth Chapel conducted a "Sabbath School," the forerunner of Catholic schools which were the pride of the North Shore. A plethora of church sponsored groups flourished, including the Edgeworth Catholic Library Association, the Edgeworth Improvement Association, the Edgeworth Literary Association, and the Edgeworth Dramatic Club. The local *Edgeworth Advocate* was a bi-weekly newspaper that reported on neighborhood and city news, as well as reporting on events in their native Ireland.

In terms of size, Edgeworth was Malden's smallest territorial ward, but its most densely populated neighborhood, maintaining about a quarter of the city's population from about 1900 to 1930. On tiny streets and courts, families lived in cramped, cold water flats, frequently sharing toilet facilities among lodgers, cellar dwellers, and those fortunate enough to afford more private quarters.

Clearly, the routine of their lives was punctuated by the tempo of their work. When there was no work, as during the severe depression of 1893, some two thousand local jobs were lost because of factory shut downs. Edgeworth's population looked for city relief and to the Church for a helping hand. But, as Richard Hofstadter observed, the cost of living skyrocketed over thirty five percent between the years 1897 and 1913, and the misery of unemployed or under-employed laborers was made endemic by an often unpredictable, inexplicable economy.[5] Trustification and other economic consolidations among the city's chief employers affected the Edgeworth economy, resulting in some plant closings, and more often, abbreviated production periods and spasmodic earnings for the demoralized workforce.

A factory...

In an earlier day, in 1900, the Boston Rubber Shoe Company was the world's largest manufacturer of rubber boots. Edgeworth enjoyed a boom. Wooden frame houses were built side by side on well laid-out streets. But in 1909 Elisha Converse abandoned his part ownership of Boston Rubber to begin his own company, the Converse Rubber Company. In 1932, Boston Rubber was gobbled up by U.S. Rubber Company. Elisha Converse's business venture was successful, but only partially so. His rubber shoe factory prospered, and his Irish and later Italian workers enjoyed relatively steady work. Although Converse was not as successful in his rubber tire business, Converse Rubber was the flagship of Malden's industries as late as 1951.

Malden's poll books from 1900 to 1932 reported the highest frequency of employment among the Edgeworth population in the

...and a nearby street

following jobs: laborers, rubber workers, teamsters, paint factory workers, tannery workers, city workers, clerks, conductors, and utility employees attesting to the blue collar nature of work among the workforce. Unmistakeably, there was an absence of a residential professional class of citizens in the Irish ward. Edgeworth provided Malden with a proletarian work force that was stable and regenerating. William Shannon has characterized Irish mobility in these years as static especially in terms of income, education, and social movement. Malden's Irish bears out Shannon's hypothesis: the persistence of blue collar occupations dominated the Ward 2 occupational workforce.[6]

Of course, the scope of this present study is not to evaluate the persistence of Irish mobility within particular occupations. What remained most impressionable, however, was the relatively low level of their jobs for the entire thirty two year period. Less than 1% of the workforce reported a professional occupation during the period under study. In all likelihood, outward migration from Ward 2 was frequent; the most financially successful of its sons and daughters made their lives outside of Malden. Initially, immigration to the ward was because of the availability of cheap housing and the opportunity for factory work. In all likelihood, Irish out-migration was due to the economic limitations of Malden. Businesses, banks, and local industry were Protestant controlled and unlikely to reward Irish-Catholic initiative. Malden's Irish never advanced in occupations or economic prominence by remaining in Edgeworth. In fact, to remain in Edgeworth was to spend a lifetime in the rubber factory or, at best, secure a scarce and infrequent niche on the city's small police or fire departments. The poll books explain where people worked, not what people desired to work at. Doubtless, existing records of Malden's major industrial and manufacturing employers are, characteristically, void of Irish manager or office personnel. One can only conclude that economic and professional advancement within the Malden firms was most limited. An examination of the annual reports of a number of Malden's most prominent firms reveal an almost totally white Anglo-Saxon managerial class. Individuals with Irish surnames rarely appear, or individuals identified as residing in the area of Ward 2 are no where to be found. Clearly, Malden's Protestant entrepreneurs did not promote Irish Catholic advancement within their firms.[7]

The poll books testify, however, that Irish women found low level secretarial employment in some of Malden's major firms. A comparison of working women listed in the post 1920 poll books of Ward 2 reveal an Irish female workforce as better than 4 to 1, compared with the city's Jewish women or any other ethnic group within the city. For the most part, Jewish women were recorded as housewives. Not only did more Irish women work, but they worked at occupations (and within businesses) that, at least today, would be perceived as possessing a "higher status" than the factory employment their husbands and sons occupied. Further, clerical workers, school teachers, and low level managerial staff distinguish the occupational profile for the women of Ward 2 at a period in time when their male counterparts appear totally restricted within the factory or the workshop.

Into the second decade of the century, the skyrocketing cost of living accounted, in part, for the large number of Irish working women. But the explosion of clerical needs for Malden's industries also necessitated the employment of women, in this case, the local Irish, especially those who could file, type, and take stenography. The mountains of paperwork generated by early twentieth century business created an inexhaustibly large task for those performing routine and static employment. This "proletarianization of clerical work" echoed the limited occupational mobility of the factory, such that both Irish men and women shared what was occupational oblivion.[8]

Local Irish women served as domestics, too. Irish servants in Yankee households were reserved for the well-to-do citizenry; there, as employees, the Irish suffered the "full measure of ethnic rancour." One of Malden's prominent families provided insight into this condition: when an Irish domestic sponsored the immigration of her brother to America, Harriet Robinson confided within her diary:

> So another one is added to the Irish population. They increase like a swarm of flies, but they are thrifty in their ways and industrious and can live on nothing and are, I think, bound to inherit the earth. It is singular, they have a foothold in every house.[9]

Whether criticizing a Bridget or a Julia, the Yankee mistress, Harriet Robinson, was "sick of the Irish - the kind we have here...I then went through the ceremony of washing my hands of the Tribe called Paddy and mentally painted on my door posts, until we are all lazier than we are now, 'No Irish need apply.'" Only more indelible than Harriet Robinson's personal prejudices was the bitter, economic fact of Irish life in Malden. No Irish will rise![10]

In the case of Ward 2, a decidedly blue-collar population advanced *vis-á-vie* the public service workforce. In fact, from 1905 through the 1920's the Malden Police Department became overwhelmingly Irish until they constituted some 90% of the force.[11] Irish lads from Malden were frequently police officers and firefighters in many of the surrounding cities and towns, too. Yankee Melrose and nearby Wilmington and Winchester could rely on a steady stream of Malden's Irish to maintain the roadways, public works departments, as well as the public utilities and railroad transit systems. In cities and towns north of Boston, Malden's Irish became

Laborers in Malden, c. 1920

the workforce for the areas ever expanding public payrolls. Nearly everyone had an Irish aunt or uncle who lived, at one time or another, in Malden's Edgeworth.

Unsurprisingly, a different occupational profile emerges for that of the Jews than from the Irish. The poll books reveal a decidedly urban and entrepreneurial disposition of Ward 7's residents. From 1912 to 1932, the ten key occupations among Malden's Jews were the following: cigar maker, salesman, bookkeeper, tailor, textile cutter, meat dealer, craftsman, carpenter, fruit peddler, and fish dealer. Twenty years later, the most prominent occupations revolved around the textile industries, fruit, meat, and produce distributors, and a huge, rather diverse body of manufacturers. Individuals involved in the knitting business, soda or tonic industry, or other varied aspects of business and industrial product development, dominate the 1932 poll records.

Besides the entrepreneurial nature of their occupations, Malden's Jewish households were headed by relatively young men and women. Households were led by couples in their thirties to early forties, individuals who sought practical results and financial rewards for their labors and for their children. They aspired to ownership or, at least, managing a share of a territorial or product market. The persistence of this occupational direction held steady for Malden Jewry well into the decade of the forties.

Malden's Jewish and Irish citizenry had little opportunity and, perhaps, inclination, to know each other. When the demands of their differing workplaces were fulfilled, each group withdrew to their respective cross town neighborhoods, families, and surroundings. The cafeterias, bakeries, coffee shops, and street corners that dotted Suffolk Square tended to be the predominant entertainment area of the Jews. Edgeworth's fraternal orders, cafes, and meeting halls bustled with activity from social gatherings to political "times", or just simple conversation among friends and neighbors.

In their work places and in their private lives, Irish and Jew were strangers to one another. No religious, educational, political, or social ties connected them, perhaps in great part because the economic direction of their employment never intersected. For example, Jews were rarely employed in Malden's older industries, such as the rubber factories; Jewish factory work was in the garment factories of Boston or in the city's largest Jewish owned and operated textile plant on the fringe of Suffolk Square. Here, the Italians worked, but not the Irish.

The Jews and the Irish had little first hand experiences or

opportunities for contact with one another, and this only heightened the anxiety and mystery each felt for one another. And yet, they undoubtedly observed one another. Malden Square was a rich and varied shopping and entertainment area, full of department and specialty stores. Trolleys converged in the square from the various neighborhoods of Malden, and it was here, too, that the trek to Boston could be made. It was in the Square where one shopped for household items, furniture, and clothing that Malden's ethnics observed one another. While the public schools, in the generations to come, introduced the Irish and the Jews to one another in a way that worked to reduce a mutual alienation, the Square remained the city's common ground for all of Malden's citizens.

Malden Square, 1928

Chapter Four

When Did It All Begin to Change?

Eyeing the camera from a livery stable, 1925

Of course, fundamental to understanding Massachusetts' politics from 1900 to 1932 were the era's ethnic fears and polarizations, which are graphically revealed in voting statistics. As the historian Richard Abrams has astutely observed, "an ethnic challenge in race conscious America (and especially Massachusetts) meant only barely less than a challenge to civilization itself."[1] Characterizing itself as the Commonwealth's last hope, the Yankee controlled Republican Party actually maintained its hegemony over both houses of the state legislature, the governorship, and the great majority of its representatives to the U.S. Congress. Republicanism boasted that it was the party of progressive reform, fiscal and governmental integrity, and utterly willing to be held accountable to the highest ethical standards of office holding. In contrast, argued Massachusetts Republicanism, the increasingly Irish led Democratic Party could neither inspire nor, indeed, convincingly portray itself as a forward looking political entity. In fact, the Democrats were frequently besmirched by ties to political bosses, cronyism, unsound economic policies and an accentuated anti-Yankee feeling which was difficult for first generation Americans to condone, understand, or wish to be associated with in any way.

Malden Jews found the Irish motivated by a quest for political revenge that Jewry found at odds with the necessary tasks of survival or, quite importantly, a constructive approach to solving the problems of cultural and societal adjustment. Ethnic slurs and stereotypes were pervasive within the political arena, frequently appealing to the most base and pernicious sentiments in the pursuit of political advantage. Demagogic appeals to racism and ethnic prejudices were perceived as dangerous and inherently dehumanizing, as Jewish history was wont to illustrate.

In fact, the Democratic Party was routinely characterized as the party of graft and political corruption, whether Irish led or under its old Yankee aegis. Especially vilified were its urban lower class followers who were characterized as out of step with traditional Massachusetts values of work, thrift, and personal integrity.

The very idea that the Boston Irish might, for instance, gain political control of Boston and its surrounding thirty nine cities and towns tormented the sensibilities of Republicans. Relatively secure, however, was Republicanism that the two million residents within the area would look to its Yankee aristocracy for political leadership. In 1883 the venerable Massachusetts Senator George Frisbie Hoar warned Cabot Lodge, however, that "the grand chapter of the old Massachusetts history is closed" unless the foreign vote could be controlled and kept out of Irish hands.[2]

Perennially, the Irish vote was Democratic, if for nothing else than to register an Irish and Catholic political protest, but the politics of protest were not the same as that of political effectiveness, or victory at the polls, or the ability to command the aura of political legitimacy. In fact, opposition to the Irish was associated with a lingering aspersion as to their societal illegitimacy, perhaps because of their religion, their economic circumstances, but mostly due to their social class. The great Irish political need, first and foremost, was to establish an awareness that Irish-led politics, and the Roman

Catholic faith, were facts of American life that could not be shunned, extinguished, or complacently denied. Perhaps it was the finality of Irish immigration to America, or the fact that few immigrant groups were so conscious of their social class, that the Irish were quite determined to resist malfeasance regardless of its guise.

In 1911, a full page advertisement appeared in *The Jewish Advocate*: "To the Voters of Massachusetts: Why it is impossible for any Jew to vote any other than the Democratic ticket in this year." The advertisement maintained that only the Democrats of Boston offered Jews political appointments and but a single Democrat in the Massachusetts House of Representatives supported Kosher slaughtering practices when a coalition of humane and vivisection groups sought to deny the practice.[3] For the most part, Democratic appeals to the Jewish vote were largely a phenomena of the large urban political arena, where political favors were commensurate with sizeable ethnic constituencies, say, for example, Boston's Jewish Wards 12 and 14.

Outside of major urban areas, the Irish were thoroughly negligent in encouraging a coalition organization.[4] In Malden and probably throughout much of the Commonwealth, the Democratic Party made no attempt to court the Jewish vote. In part, this was due to the fact that Malden's Jewish life was relegated, almost entirely, within the Suffolk Square area of Ward 7; it seems that even political contact between the Democratic Party and the Jews was a less than desirable proposition. In Malden, the Democratic city committee was without a Jewish member till nearly 1936. Newspaper reports of the local Democratic organization establish that the Party was an Irish-led and constituted body that looked at Democratic politics as "Irish Nights," and under their exclusive control.[5]

As a case in point, in 1928, Malden's Al Smith Club in Ward 7 was led by the Ward's Irish residents, with not a single Jewish sponsor, irrespective of the Jewish domination in the ward and the fact, demonstrated by the electoral results of that election, that Jewish support for Smith's candidacy was of an enormous magnitude in Malden and throughout the nation.[6] Heedless of the fact that Smith's candidacy brought ethnic peoples together in his 1928 elective bid, the Malden Democratic Party did not encourage either building coalitions or sharing the political reins. As such, 1928 did not witness an actual Jewish participation within the Democratic Party organization, although Smith's candidacy clearly demonstrated the depth of electoral potential within an ethnic political coalition. Doubtless, the 1928 campaign demonstrated that not only the Irish vote mattered and needed to be taken seriously, but that other ethnics, too, possessed a latent political strength.

Just as Malden's Democratic Party appeared oblivious to the electoral need for coalition building, the Republican Party, too, struggled with the notion that it should court ethnic voters, and

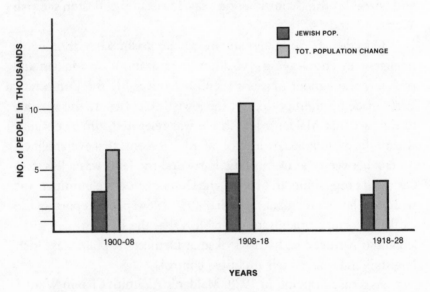

Chart 1   Jewish Population and Population Change in the City

instead, presumed Jewish political support. This proved increasingly annoying to the Jewish community.

As Malden's Jewish population mushroomed in size, the earlier liberal tone of "the free-thinking" Deliberative Society took on a more parochial, strained tone. The Society rejected the image of America as a refuge for persecuted Jews suffering pogroms and genocide. America besieged became the more pertinent simile, especially as Ward 7 assumed a decidedly Jewish character.[7]

The local press informed readers that in 1904, an entire section of Ward 7 was almost entirely populated by Jews.[8] Indeed, it baited its readers by suggesting that the Jews were invading the city's neighborhoods, and that too many Jewish children were in the public schools.[9] Were all the Jewish children of Russia to be educated in Malden, the local press queried?

The once rural intersection of town that was Suffolk Square became full of people, bustling and teeming with foot-traffic, horse draw wagons, and even an electrified trolley connection to Boston's Elevated Railway. Painted on the storefront windows were signs in Hebrew advertising kosher meat markets and restaurants that would indelibly mark the area as Jewish for the next fifty years. On the sidewalks one could hear the expressive Yiddish of the passersby and shopowners that subjugated English as a foreign tongue. Among Malden's more native population, a popular, somewhat rhetorical, question arose, almost as a kind of local trivia: when was it that the first Jew appeared in Malden? Many of Malden's most esteemed citizens, its authors and historians, were both fascinated by the growth of Malden's Jewish population as well as aghast that their city became home to such a large number of Jews.[10]

Local Republicans looked upon the Jewish residents as a necessary but essentially alien constituency in Malden's future development. Tax valuations for the Suffolk Square area bolstered the city's gross property valuations, and, in fact, the city's property valuations exhibited an upward, economic burst due to its Jewish population. Malden's downtown shopping area gradually received a boost from the Jewish neighborhood shoppers, and its resultant economic expansion made Malden the area's prime commercial center north of Boston.[11] However, this is not to say that the city fathers were especially proud of Malden Jewry. Quite the contrary.

In the summer of 1912, for example, President William Howard Taft made a campaign swing through Malden hoping to maintain the traditional Republican strongholds, but it was to little avail; Malden was very much Teddy Roosevelt territory.

Nonetheless, the President received a warm and rather festive greeting with the city going to lavish ends to entertain the President with a huge banquet and testimonial for five thousand guests. A parade through the main thoroughfares of the city occurred, and the city's school-aged children were encouraged to greet the President,

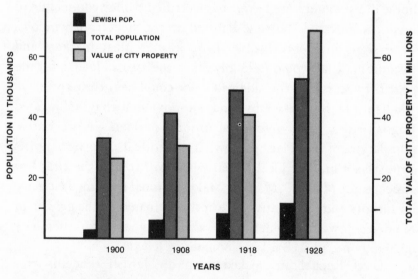

Chart 2   Jews and the City's Economic Growth

waving flags and singing patriotic songs. However, not only did the parade circumvent the Jewish quarter, but no Jewish residents participated as part of the community's representation committee. Despite the fact that the banquet list of dignitaries and other participants included the religious leaders of Malden, the affair proceeded without a representative of the Jewish community. "I remember my father among those at the parade route, for he held me up to see the President," recalled Rabbi Boruchoff's daughter.

In truth, whenever the city engaged in civic tributes or public undertakings, the Jewish residents were scrupulously avoided as guests and never invited as participants. The Jewish presence was considered just too exotic and perhaps alien, and Malden's city fathers thought it best that Jewish life be excluded from the city's celebrative moments.

Be that as it may, the summer of 1912 was a significant time for many Jews in Malden, for that was when its Jewish residents were conducting a city wide boycott of Kosher meat markets after the citizenry experienced an increase of some 50% in their meat costs. Five hundred Jewish women in Malden were active participants in policing the meat boycott and supporting larger efforts of consumer consciousness. A twenty-one year old housewife, Eva Hoffman, led a progressive and humanitarian cry for social change during that steamy New England summer of 1912.

> This is a struggle for the women and children who are underfed. The meat that sold for 16 cents is now selling for 25 cents. The poor housewife who is obliged to make both ends meet is able to buy meat only for the head of the family while she and her children starve.

Jewish life in Malden was noticably avoided during Taft's visit, but especially when public demonstrations, open-air meetings, and a

An elderly Russian Jew

...reunited with his daughter in America, c. 1920

degree of physical violence punctuated the Jewish quarter.[12]

The eminent historian of American political reform, Richard Hofstadter, believed that "consumer consciousness became a thing of much significance because it was the lowest common denominator among classes of people who had little else to unite them on concrete issues."[13] Not so, apparently, in Malden. The Yankee middle class possessed little sympathy for economic conditions affecting the poor, the Irish, or immigrant Jews. Perhaps in a larger city, such as New York or Boston, an urban boss would have taken advantage of this discontent for the *quid pro quo* of political support. This did not occur here. Instead, the problems of the Jews were the exclusive concern of them alone. Indeed, neither the urban boss nor Malden's progressives came to aid or join the local Jews in a larger political covenant. Nonetheless, only when the political history of the period is scrutinized through its electoral record, can one assess the ethnic impetus to Massachusetts' political culture.

Chapter Five

Short Measure

Laying of the YMCA cornestone, 1895

A pronounced Jewish support for Teddy Roosevelt existed as early as 1895 when he was Police Commissioner in New York. "When the notorious German anti-Semite, Pastor Hermann Ahlwardt, arrived in New York to address a large public meeting, the Police Commissioner with tongue in cheek assigned only Jewish policemen to protect him."[1] Roosevelt was often credited for his outspoken protest against Jewish pogroms in Russia and Rumania. In fact, most American Jews appreciated Presidents McKinley, Roosevelt, Taft, and Wilson because they did not actively deter Jewish emigration to the United States.

Teddy Roosevelt was much admired by reform Republicans, and especially by Malden's Progressive Party. Yankee Republican support for Teddy Roosevelt was enthusiastic and outspoken.

> . . . there is no one that revered Lincoln more than me — so much that I named my first born after him, giving him a middle name in honor of Wm. A. Gladstone, who also was a great commoner. Yet I consider Theodore Roosevelt a greater man than Lincoln was. The Theodore Roosevelt of today is working to free the white slaves as Lincoln did the Black. Not that all

men are white slaves but the political conditions make many of them so. I want to testify to the great love I have for Roosevelt.[2]

On September 13, 1912 at the Malden YMCA, some twenty speakers rose to pay homage to Teddy Roosevelt. Jewish support for Teddy Roosevelt was overwhelming in Malden despite the fact that no single Jew was listed in the local press as a political supporter or operative for the Progressive Party.[3] The visibility of Jewish social concerns and the Jewish political record are brought to light, however, by an analysis of the Jewish voting record.

The raw vote percentages for the Jewish vote in Ward 7 and the Irish vote in Ward 2, Malden's ethnically sanitized voting districts, are presented for nine presidential contests and some twenty-seven gubernatorial elections.[4] In general, they support the contention (shown in Figure 1) that the Irish vote was a solidly Democratic vote, while the Jewish vote was very much Republican, with generally

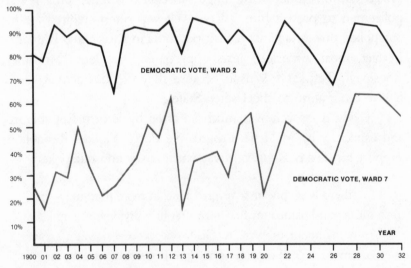

Figure 1   Democratic Vote by Year, Wards 2 and 7

under one-third of the Jewish votes cast going to Democrats. In any presidential election year, there is ticket-splitting with some voting for the Presidential candidate of one party and the gubernatorial candidate of the other party. Rather than voting a straight party ticket, ticket-splittings suggest that a degree of assessment has occurred, especially over a period of time when clear electoral patterns emerge. That is, considerations of candidates' positions can be measured and party platforms can be assessed. This willingness to vote without regard for party consistency or any other political adherence was clearly evident in Jewish voting. Political discernment characterized their electoral decision making.

One indication of the independence of Ward 7 voters is apparent when ticket-splitting is explored. To provide an indication of "baseline" ticket-splitting, Ward 7 can be compared to the Irish Ward 2 in Figure 2. This figure shows the absolute value of ticket-splitting; that is, it shows the percentage of voters in each ward who split their vote. This chart shows significantly more independence in

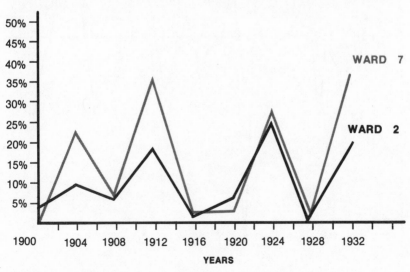

Figure 2   Percent of Voters Splitting Tickets

81

Ward 7 than in Ward 2. If we allow for a nominal amount of ticket-splitting in any election (say, 10%) then before 1932, there were two election periods in which Ward 2 did significant ticket-splitting, while Ward 7 showed wide splits in three of the eight potential elections. More significantly, from 1900 to 1932, the Jewish voters in Ward 7 split their ticket more often than the Irish voters in Ward 2 in seven of the nine elections. (In the other two elections, Ward 2 ticket-splitting was greater by 3.8% to 1.1% in 1900, and by 5.1% to 3.6% in 1920, both results are at an insignificant level.)

A better indication of the degree of independence of Jewish voters in Malden is the swing from year to year in voting patterns.

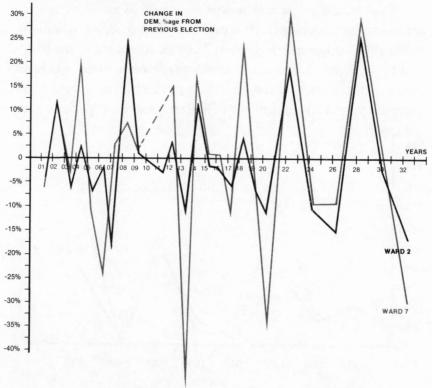

Figure 3   Change in Percentage Total for Democratic Candidate

This provides twenty-six data points rather than merely nine. Figure 3 shows the change in the percentage vote for the Democratic gubernatorial candidate from election to election in the two wards. For example, in 1901, Ward 2 gave 77.6% of its vote to the Democratic candidate. In 1902, the Democratic candidate received 93.9% of Ward 2's vote. This is shown in Figure 3 as a jump of 16.3 percentage points from 1901 to 1902. In other words, if there were 1000 voters in Ward 2, 163 who did not vote Democratic in 1901 did vote Democratic in 1902. That is, they changed the party for which they voted. Figure 3 shows wider swings in Ward 7, that is, greater independence in switching parties from election to election. In fourteen of twenty-four elections, the swing in Ward 7's vote exceeded the swing in Ward 2's vote, demonstrating once again a different, yet discernable, voting profile for both wards. Irish bloc voting and Jewish independent voting differentiate their respective electoral records.

Another way at looking at the degree of independence in the two wards is taking the average vote over the entire time span, and

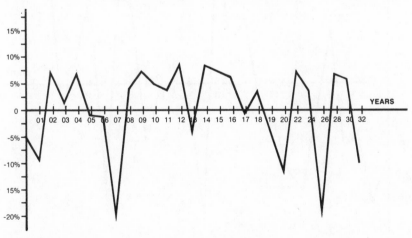

Figure 4   Deviation from Average Democratic Vote in 27 Elections, Ward 2

then examining the deviation from that average over time. In the twenty-seven gubernatorial elections from 1900 to 1932, the average Democratic vote in Ward 2 was 86.8%; as mentioned previously, in Ward 7 it was 39.3%. Figures 4 and 5 show the deviation from the average Democratic vote in these two wards. The far greater swings in Ward 7 are evident, as might be expected. The wider swings of Ward 7 corroborate the ward's voting independence, and again establish a discernible voting pattern.[5] In fact, the absolute value of the deviations average 6.7 for Ward 2 and 12.1 for Ward 7. The thirty-two year average of the swings of the Democratic vote were twice as great in Ward 7, another sign of independent voting.

Another view of Figure 1 indicates that the fortunes of Democratic candidates rose and fell in both wards together, although the much higher base of support in Ward 2 elevates that Democratic

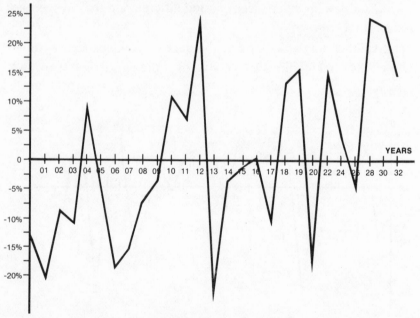

Figure 5   Deviation from Average Democratic Vote in 27 Elections, Ward 7

margin. Candidates were likely to attract swing voters in both wards. Shifting the scale, as in Figure 6, shows that Democratic candidates generally had the same relative attraction in the two wards. The scale of Figure 6 gives Democratic candidates a base of solid support from 35% of Ward 2 voters. This demonstrates a coincidence of interest among swing voters in both ethnic communities. Increasingly, the Jewish voters began to cast their ballots like the heavily Catholic Ward 2 from as early as 1913 and continuing through 1930. As such, the 1928 Al Smith coalition was less a breakthrough and more a culmination of a fifteen year electoral trend, at least in the case of Malden Jewry, that probably was related to certain identifiable political and social circumstances, which we shall examine. Figure 7

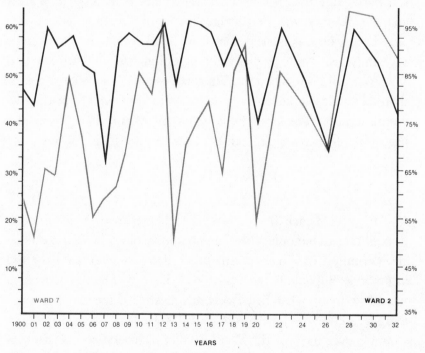

Figure 6   Democratic Vote in Wards 2 and 7

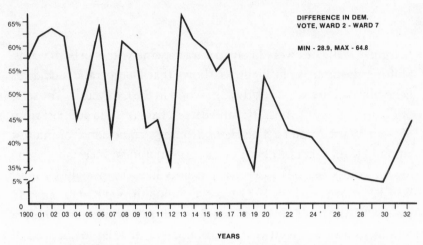

Figure 7   Differences Between Democratic Vote Percentages, Ward 2 - Ward 7

shows the difference between the Democratic percentage in Ward 2 and the Democratic percentage in Ward 7. Although a wide difference exists, it is clear that from 1913, when the Democratic vote in Ward 2 was 64.8 percentage points higher than it was in Ward 7, until 1930, when the difference was 28.9 percentage points, there is an almost unbroken trend toward convergence of the two voting groups. Electorally, the years 1918 and 1919 mark the beginning of increased agreement between the Irish and Jews.

In fact, Malden Jewry grew disenchanted with Massachusetts Republicanism but only when Republican ideology proved hostile to any definition of Americanism other than its own. In 1910 the incumbent Republican governor was Eban S. Draper, serving a second term of what had frequently been a three term tenure.[6] Draper received the Jewish vote in his 1909 bid for the governorship, winning over 63% of the Ward 7 vote. In his 1908 gubernatorial campaign, he won 68% of the ward. In nearby Ward 2, Draper tallied but a scant average of 7.7% of the ward's vote in three electoral efforts, in part since on two occasions his Democratic opponent was an Irishman, James H. Vahey. In fact, Draper's plurality in the 1908-1909 campaign was a slight 6000 votes. Draper was a successful businessman and textile manufacturer from Hopedale, Massachusetts, and typical of most Republican standard-bearers in terms of wealth and affiliation to the business community.

But he shared little of the patrician radicalism or the sense of civic improvement which characterized many who had preceded him, and especially the reform administration of his predecessor, Governor Curtis Guild.[7] Boston's Louis Brandeis was on a "My dear Curtis" basis with Guild, because of both men's commitment to social reform. Brandeis' renowned Savings Bank Life Insurance plan was signed into law by Governor Guild. Unlike Guild, Draper was a stand-pat politican and a stubborn man who glossed over questions of social justice or political equity in Massachusetts; in fact, he was not oblivious to the Republican Party's reform rhetoric and agenda. But he was a formidable politician due to his wealth, his reputation as a no-nonsense industrialist, and a political acumen regarding the citizenry's frustrations with immigrant radicalism, labor unrest, and the spectre of social upheaval.

But Draper's popularity ebbed in the 1910 contest, although he ran against an ex-Republican, recently turned Progressive-Democrat named Eugene Foss. After two terms in office, and challenged by the maverick personage of Foss, Draper was exposed for what he truly was: vapid, arrogant, and as Richard Abrams has perceptively noted, "dim-sighted."[8]

Draper was defeated by Foss in 1910 with Foss capturing 52% of the Commonwealth's total vote. Among Malden's Jews, Draper received his lowest percentage of a three term voter turnout, less than 49% of the vote, but a plummeting of nearly twenty percentage points lower than his 1908 turnout. It has been argued that in 1908 a vote for Draper was perceived as a vote against the Irish. By 1910, a vote against Draper bordered on a vote against Draper's ideology, and many other Republicans' provincial interpretation of Americanism, including a primitive understanding of the rights of working people, and an ethnocentric belief that economic opportunity and Anglo-Saxonism were mutually inclusive.

What Draper failed to appreciate about reform and Republicanism was more than compensated for by his popular appeal to prejudice and xenophobia, and utter mistrust of cultural pluralism. In 1910 the Jews of Ward 7 turned away from Draper's ideology for a number of important reasons that help illuminate Jewish political consciousness of the period.

For example, Draper signed into law the Boston Railroad Holding Company Act of 1909 which allowed for the merger of the Boston and Maine and the New Haven Railroads. By doing so, Draper knuckled under to the moneyed trusts controlled by the financial empires of Morgan and Mellon. The subsequent decline of railroad services and a host of well-publicized stock frauds tarnished the reputations of all involved in the "Draper Bill."

Louis Brandeis was the legal and political pointman who fought the railroad merger until its ultimate passage. The evils of the merger mania and the neglect of the public's rights for efficient and competitive public services made Brandeis a champion to many Progressives, and especially Jews who were proud of his political prominence and social activism.[9]

Draper lost the confidence of Malden's Jews for reasons, however, that grew out of both statewide events as well as specific local problems affecting the Jewish community. In 1909 and 1910, the Massachusetts General Court passed Eight-Hour Laws, attempts to regulate and humanize the workplace, only to have Draper twice veto the legislation. Also in 1909, the Governor denounced some 1500 Polish workers in a jute mill in the western Massachusetts town of Ludlow for engaging in a long and tenacious strike. Similarly,

Draper denounced the shoe workers of Brockton when they challenged wage cuts in 1909-1910. All in all, Draper alienated working people and ethnic people. He associated ethnicity with anti-capitalism and even anti-Americanism, especially when the industrial network to which he was so integrally associated was under seige. Law and order was jeopardized, Draper argued, when immigrants were allowed to walk away from their workbenches, especially under the aegis of "radical doctrine" which, he declared, was inimicable to American life. Doubtless, Draper's anti-immigrant feelings were predicated on his mission of single-handedly preserving those businesses that remained indifferent to the plight of thousands of laborers that helped the free market achieve its success.

Malden Jewry was disappointed that the Governor made such unfortunate and ethnically prejudicial judgments that alienated even the staunchest supporters of the Republican cause. In effect, Draper made Jews alert to immigrant baiting. In addition, Malden's Jews were sensitive to politicians who brandished an ideology predicated upon the denigration of working class citizens.

During Draper's tenure the Massachusetts Commission on Immigration published *The Problem of Immigration in Massachusetts*, focusing particularly upon the rising crime rates in cities with large immigrant populations. In part, Draper's anti-immigrant vindictives probably inspired the recommendations for stricter enforcement of laws associated with immigrant lawbreakers.

In Malden, this was a sore subject and especially onerous upon local Jews. Malden police records reveal that record numbers of arrests occurred for a variety of "Jewish" offenses. Suffolk Square, in effect, was identified as the Jewish crime center of Malden, and local Jewry was characterized as corrupt and profligate. "Jewish crime" was invariably associated with infractions of codes or ordinances in the operation of small business. In his classic study of New York Jews, Moses Rischin ably captured the circumstances surrounding the Jewish lawbreaker of New York but his words could well have been of Malden, too.

> The violations of the law that characterized the immigrant community . . . were an outgrowth of occupational overcrowding, poverty, and religious habits.... Concentrated in marginal commerce and industry, Jews transgressed the codes of commercial law. 'The prevalence of a spirit of enterprise out of proportion to the capital of the community' gave rise to a higher incidence of felonious larceny, forgery, and failure to pay wages. Peddlers and petty shopkeepers were especially vulnerable to police oppression for evading informal levies as well as formal licensing requirements. Legislation controlling business on Sunday found Jewish immigrants natural victims. In so congested a district, the breaking of corporation ordinances was unavoidable and the slaughtering of chickens in tenements in violation of the sanitary code proved to be a distinctly Jewish infraction. [10]

In Malden, business crime became synonymous with Jewish crime. As such, Jews were quite angered by elected officials such as Draper who labelled them a bad element within the community, and a danger to the Commonwealth.

In point of fact, Malden Jewry was subject to extraordinary police scrutiny and surveillance. In a thirty two year analysis of arrest records, some 30,000 offenses were recorded in the Malden Police logs. By analyzing an arrestee's surname, national origin, residence, and occupation, it is possible to be reasonably certain as to the

Jacob Goodman	8.08 P.m.	Russia	White	Male	26	Dark
Frank Soloman	8.08 P.m.	Russia	"	"	19	Dark
Morris Goodman	808 P.m.	"	"	"	20	Dark
Abram Leomas	808 P.m.	U.S.	"	"	20	Dark
Samuel Winer	808 P.m.	U.S.	"	"	15	Dark
Max Norman	808 P.m.	Eng.	"	"	17	Dark
George Blume	808 P.m.	U.S.	"	"	16	Dark
Benjamin Axelrod	808 P.m.	U.S.	"	"	15	Dark
Isreal Himelfarb	840 P.m.	Eng.	"	"	19	Med.
Jacob L. Rubitzky	840 P.m.	Russia	"	"	18	Sandy
Patrick Connors	9.30 P.m.	Ire.	"	"	52	Med.
Albert Gordon	4.50	Russia	"	"	42	Dark
Nicholas Naun	11-10	Gret	"	"	30	Med
Harry McGaffigan	5.25 G.M	Ire	"	"	40	Med
Julia Owens	843 P.m.	Ire.	"	Female	40	Med.
Thomas H. Martin	12.30 a.m.	U.S.	"	Male	27	Gray
Boyd J. Gates	5.45 A.M	Ue.S.	"	"	15	Med
Peter McDonough	11- a-m	Ire	"	"	53	Med
Patrick J. Fogarty	11.40 P.m.	Ire.	"	"	27	Med.
Costas Bournaros	10.40 aur. Athens Greece		"	"	20	"

Sample from the Malden Police Department Arrest Books for 1909 individual being either Jew or Gentile. As in New York, Malden's Jews were arrested for certain distinct offenses. In 1917, Jews constituted some 95% of those arrested for violation of the fowl laws or the sale of liquor to minors. According to the arrest records, Jews were responsible for 92% of all violations regarding the sale of liquor in the community from about 1921 through 1932. Those arrested for selling without a license, giving short measure, forging, and a variety of other "business" or "entrepreneurial" crimes were invariably Jews.[11]

To the Jews of Ward 7, these arrests were a clear indication not of their criminality, but of the social and cultural adjustments of American life. In a small city, Jews could not be "lost" in the tumult and human activity or general populousness of, say, New York. In the small city, Jewish infractions found their way into the police logs,

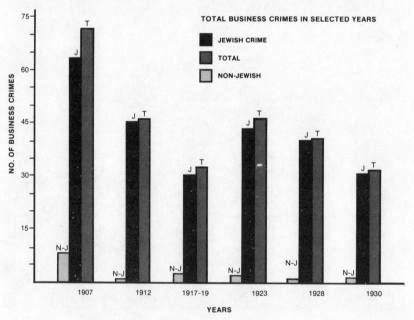

Chart 3   Total Business Crimes in Selected Years

because there existed a willingness to arrest Jews. Living conditions within the tenements of Ward 7 were frequently cramped, squalid, and unsanitary. Numerous individuals performed the services of plumbers, electricians, carpenters, and mechanics for friends as well as for fees, despite local ordinances. Regulations regarding milk laws, the measure of goods, and other codes affecting small businesses were annoyances to the local community. Indeed, the Jewish community often believed that local regulations and their enforcement were merely a convenience for, what was in fact, harassment. Many ordinances annoyed local Jews because of their arbitrary enforcement by the Malden Police because Suffolk Square was a ready site for plenty of arrests. Since the Malden Police force consisted of mainly Irish Catholics, Irish versus Jewish resentment necessarily occurred.

In addition, Malden's Jews did not possess the financial resources or social experience to litigate and challenge the local police. Those individuals arrested were predominantly males between the ages of 20 and 50 years old who were aspiring entrepreneurs interested in or operating small enterprises. Most of the arrests involved fairly young, family-oriented individuals. As noted earlier, the community was overwhelmingly Orthodox in religion. Such individuals considered zealous law enforcement an ethnic and religious assault as well as a challenge to Jewish business ambitions.[12]

This was evident by Jewish disregard for Massachusetts Blue Laws in which business activities and specified recreation were prohibited on Sunday. What became a legal problem, arrest and fines for working and even participating in Sunday sports events, was actually *cultural crime*. Malden was home to some five Orthodox synagogues between 1904 and 1932 with a religiously conscious and faithful population, or at least, a Jewish population respectful of other Jews, and especially respectful of the Jewish Sabbath.

Yet the police arrests for the operation of Jewish owned Sunday business persisted through the 1920's. It was clear to Jew and Gentile alike that Suffolk Square was the target of the enforcement of the Blue Laws. According to the *Malden News* on May 28, 1915:

> An Attorney of note says, that many of the laws about Sunday opening are unconstitutional, but the new order to enforce them affects only poor store keepers who are not able to contest. The Suffolk Square section is the hardest hit.[13]

Unfamiliarity in a new land, the unwillingness to litigate over police harassment, problems over legal fees, and many other considerations concerning police-Jewish relations underscore Jewish criminality more than the arrest records reveal. Of course, the Jewish community did not support those individuals who pursued a life of corruption. Yet it was clear to the Jews they were being singled out for arrest. As a case in point, selling without a license or providing a service without a license were frequent offenses by Jews in 1907. Such offenses nearly disappear by 1917 and 1918. Prior to the Jewish presence in the city, the offence rarely appeared in the records, also. Without Jewish arrestees, the regulation lapsed into an antiquated offense. The Malden police arrested Jews for offenses the police looked for exclusively in the Jewish community but, apparently, nowhere else in the city. Indeed, "business" crime became synonymous with Jewish crime.

Chapter Six

A Tiny Riot in 1911

Family picture, 1910

That both Malden and the Commonwealth were prejudiced toward Jews was readily observable to the Malden Jews in an even more specific way. Local Jews were, in fact, discriminated against in terms of serving on juries in Malden and probably throughout most small cities and towns in Massachusetts. Jews, in fact, were systematically excluded from selection as a jurors by Malden officials, and in effect by county and state officials, too, for over three decades.[1]

Dated July 13, 1912, the *Malden News* reported an incensed meeting by Ward 7 Jews due to their exclusion from juror lists, and as a result, their less than complete enfranchisement.[2]

The juror lists were published on a yearly basis in the local newspapers, but without a recognizable Jewish surname or address from 1900 through the early 1930's. Indeed, Attorney Raphael Boruchoff spearheaded the Jewish protest. Boruchoff recognized that the Jews of Malden were prevented from serving on juries, and had been for as long as the lists were assembled by the local registrar of voters. Boruchoff brought his charges of institutional anti-Semitism before the press, public forums, and finally before the Massachusetts Legislature. He appeared before the Rules

Committee of the House of Representatives charging Malden with excluding Jews from its juror system.

In Malden the voting lists are prepared by the Registrar of Voters. As long as I can remember and as long as any other resident of Malden with whom I have spoken can remember, the name of a citizen of the Jewish persuasion has never been known to be on a jury list. . . . The same condition, I am told, is true throughout the county of Middlesex. . . such jury lists do not give us a jury of our peers. . . . I sincerely hope that your committee will recommend the creation of a commission that will not disenfranchise a people.[3]

As early as 1920, the Legislature of Massachusetts established at least two commissions to study and appraise the entire judicial system so as to improve its efficiency and modernize its chaotic financing and system of organization. Two major reports were prepared for consideration by the members of the House and Senate Judiciary Committees.[4]

Included in its deliberation was a special charge concerning the question of juror eligibility. In Boston, for example, a great controversy involved the judgment of the city's Election Commissioners in establishing the jury list with the exclusion of Boston women. But neither the subject of jury service for women or minorities was felt to be within the purview of the established Judicature Commissions; as a result, jury composition was avoided in the final reports of both investigative committees.

Certainly, Boruchoff's charges were accepted as testimony before the Rules Committee, but nothing else was done. The preparation of voting lists was believed to be a local matter, best left to the citizens and government of Malden. In addition, discrimination — whether actual or merely alleged — was viewed as a social ill. The Judicature Commission's concerns were with the organization, finance and administration, and operation of the courts.[5] In fact, another fifty years would pass before the Massachusetts court system would be overhauled.

As for jury list discrimination against Malden's Jews and, possibly, most Jews in Massachusetts, neither the appointed Judicature Committees or the duly elected members of the Judiciary committee gave credence to Boruchoff's charges.

Robert Grant, Judge of Probate for Suffolk County, commented on the conditions within the Massachusetts "Bench and Bar" in Albert Hart's magisterial *Commonwealth History of Massachusetts.* Grant's remarks regarding "Race Elements in the Bar" are illuminating, especially in terms of his advice to individuals such as Boruchoff

> Prior to 1889, the lawyers of the Commonwealth, except for a considerable number of Irish extraction, were of the so-called native stock, and their characteristics might be said to have been homogeneous. The admission to the bar of capable and trustworthy representatives of Italian, and a little later of Jewish, birth or extraction provided litigants, who were newcomers and unable to speak English, with the means of protection, and their pioneer advisers with a renumerative livelihood. This service speedily encouraged imitation and then competition, partly to meet a genuine need and partly from racial pride.[6]

It was logical for Jewish lawyers to represent Jewish litigants, or as Grant expressed it, attorneys "of their own blood."[7] That Jewish jurors might also be desirable from a legal viewpoint, aside from an exercise of their American citizenship, was either ignored or taken for granted.

The final result was, however, that Malden Jews were prevented from serving on juries with neither elected officials or social reformers questioning what was viewed as a local prerogative. Change was slow in coming. It was not until the middle 1930's that Jewish jurors served on a Middlesex county jury. If the condition of their legal rights was an index of Massachusetts' ethnic climate, the Jews of Malden recognized that their rights, civil or political, were not going to be championed by anyone but themselves. In particular, the rhetoric of both political parties as regards equal opportunity or sharing of political partnership clashed resoundingly with the reality of Massachusetts' life.

Publicly, neither Democrats nor Republicans went out of their way for the rights of Jews and Jews recognized that their existence within the city and state possessed an element of *stethl*-like life. The selective enforcement of the law alienated the greater Jewish community from the police and, indeed, from an overall judical process that perceived Jews to be less than acceptable citizens. Long before the decade of the 1920's sought to prohibit further Jewish immigration to America, cities such as Malden apparently planned to isolate and circumvent Jewish-American rights.

At about 8:30 p.m. on Sunday July 23, 1911, an estimated forty young men converged on Suffolk Square. The riot that followed left no one dead, but nearly two dozen men and women had been beaten and an entire community had been terrorized, assaulted, and left trembling with the kind of fear that America was not supposed to engender, or so they had believed. The youths were aged seventeen through their early twenties, and their names evinced their Irish ancestory. Although it remains unclear as to exactly what prompted the events which occurred on that evening, social and political significance of that event convinced the local Jews that the most fundamental flaws existed within the social fibre of their adopted city; while not exactly a "pogrom", the Jews believed that prejudice was their constant, even historical companion, and that life in Malden would be no exception. Now blood and violence invaded their American homes. With shouts of "Beat the Jews" and "Kill the Jews . . . Get them, get them, death to all these Jews," the two central arteries to Suffolk Square witnessed the shattering of the quiet of that late Sunday dusk before what seemed a horde of charging men armed with iron bars, wagon spokes, stones, and jagged-edged bottles. Grocery and meat market windows were smashed and broken glass was everywhere.

Four out of an estimated forty young men were arrested that evening. Another sixteen individuals were later indicted. Throughout the Jewish neighborhood, the assault dominated the conversation and consciousness of the residents. The next morning throngs of people entered Suffolk Square not only to do their early week's business or household shopping, but also to examine the evidence of the night before. Broken bottles littered the street and sidewalks, traces of blood from bleeding faces and skulls stained storefront pavements. Speaking in Yiddish, the expressions of "Beating Jews" and "Killing Jews" echoed through the neighborhood, producing a haunting, disquieting feeling that was seemingly ancient and, perhaps, quite Jewish. Was there to be no peace, even in America, they wondered? Was there no refuge?

Arguing before a packed courtroom presided over by Malden District Judge Preble, H.I. Morrison, attorney for the Jewish community, patiently, methodically, but with alternating moments of extraordinary passion, articulated the circumstances concerning the anti-Jewish assault. Morrison was a lifelong Republican, a man who had worked both as an attorney and a social reformer for justice and social equity. But in his presentation of this case, he underscored a number of troubling integral problems regarding Jewish life in Malden, and indeed, in America.

Morrison maintained that this attack was only part of a long-standing, pre-concerted plan to terrorize and even extinguish the Jewish population of Malden; that the Jews of Malden were deliberately and consciously assaulted because they were Jews, and that Jews were considered second class citizens, and a proper target for both organized terror and institutional neglect. Indeed, Morrison argued, the Malden Police Department was and remained hostile to the Jewish community. The police were intentionally slow in responding to the attack, and had consistently under-staffed police protection for the area. In fact, the police officers and the police command sympathized with the gang of toughs and, indeed, encouraged the violence to take its course. Morrison informed Judge Preble that these were not merely his judgements, but the collective beliefs of the Jewish community and that, as their spokesperson, the Jewish people of Malden had lost confidence in the police as their protectors. The police and the entire city government had no respect for Jewish property and life, and that the fate of Malden's Jewish community was uncertain and perhaps doomed.

Before a packed, mostly Jewish courtroom crowd, Morrison produced witness after witness attesting to the violence and bloodshed of the assault, the cries of anti-Semitism, the negligence of the police, and the feelings of utter helplessness of Malden's Jews as they witnessed the actions of both the perpetrators and the conspiratorial police. The Jews were incensed but they were even more perplexed as to the implications of their adopted city being in collusion with their tormentors.

During that first week, a mass meeting was conducted at

Foresters Hall, Suffolk Square, and a number of resolutions were adopted by the community calling for real police protection, actual concern by the local officials, and punishment to those found guilty. The press reported that "resolutions were adopted to the affect that the rioting was unprovoked, that police protection in Suffolk Square was inadequate and inefficient for the large territory, and that better protection be afforded."[8] More pointed dissatisfaction also surfaced. "It was also charged that the police did not respond promptly to this call of Sunday evening and that they went into this case in a half-hearted way. Malden's Mayor Fall was criticized for not taking more interest in the Jewish people."[9] Malden's plan, according to Attorney Morrison and many other Malden Jews, was to stop Jews from making the city their home, or to discourage Jews from believing that Malden welcomed them, or afforded them the security, serenity, or economic opportunity that a booming Suffolk Square suggested was but a hint of what America might offer.

Captain Foley of the Malden Police Department disagreed with Morrison's assessment of the case. Foley stated that, "He didn't believe the gang was going to beat up the Jews."[10] This was not an assault, he argued, but a problem blown out of proportion by the Jewish community. Foley suggested that the fight in Suffolk Square was an isolated event that was not inherently anti-Semitic; more importantly, the perpetrators, or the "Marsh lads" as they were identified by the local paper, were rowdy but fine Maldonians.[11]

It was further argued by Captain Foley that the police were not negligent in arresting the perpetrators and that the police would vigorously prosecute the case.

Through Henry Morrison, Malden Jewry petitioned the court to prevent the police from presenting the facts of the case, arguing that the police were insensitive to and incapable of representing the Jewish community. Morrison maintained that the community desired that he present the facts of the case, and that the community, through its spokesman, be allowed to appear before the court. The Judge agreed despite the protest of the Malden police and Malden officialdom. Meeting on numerous occassions that summer, the Jewish community voiced their distrust of the police and the court, too.

Weeks of delay occurred due to the frequent requests of Peter McGuire, attorney for a group of the defendants, who sought and received a myriad of continuances. In fact, numerous other delays were petitioned for and received by the defense throughout the remainder of the summer. Through it all, the Jewish community waited and watched.

Twenty individuals were ultimately arraigned. On August 9, 1911, a first full day of testimony occurred. Defendants argued that they were the ones set upon by "old men with whiskers" and whatever violence that occurred was as a result of the Jews. No one could know, the youths argued, what was on the mind of Malden's Jews.

The prosecution, under Morrison's charge, explained that a plot to "kill the Jews" and "Beat the Jews" was intentionally employed to intimidate, harass, and indeed, injure the Jewish community. Hate and anti-Semitism, Morrison argued, fomented this riot, and the entire Malden community knew it to be the case. The assault was a mere symptom of deeper, more integral anti-Jewish feeling that was harbored within the city. A half dozen days of additional testimony and deliberations followed.

Only the four individuals arrested on the night of the disturbance would be found guilty, each paying a fifty dollar fine. The court continued without a finding for the other defendants, and the case was finished. The Jewish community felt abused by both the crime and now the punishment. Justice failed. Malden failed. Prejudice and injustice prevailed, just as they had in the countless villages and ghettoes from which they had come. A question took root in the minds of many Jews in Malden: what was the cause of this American anti-Semitism that poised poor Gentiles against poor Jews? Jews such as Boruchoff and Morrison began to believe both the victims and the criminals were pawns in a larger, more complex struggle.

The Malden court was the third largest court in the Commonwealth and it had been known as the most important of the Commonwealth's District Courts. Up until the judicial appointment of Judge Lawrence Brooks in 1928, the Malden Court was the home of an infinite number of Special Justices who served as part-time judges, with a daily schedule as brief as from 9:00 to 11:00 A.M., and who performed their duties without ardor and, often times, without civility. Indeed, one such Special Justice referred to his colleagues in Malden and similar district courts as "the lowest form of judicial vermine" interested in the court associated connections that such judgeships nurtured.[12]

Certainly from 1900 up until the appointment of the most competent Judge Brooks, the quality of the Malden court was so low that in 1924 Governor Alvin Fuller's first order of judicial business was "to cleanse the Malden Court."[13] From 1903 to 1927, the Malden District Court was nominally presided over by Charles Bruce. Brooks referred to Bruce's tenure in Malden as a period when "the reputation of the court [had] dropped to a very low ebb . . . I don't know how he (Governor Fuller) got rid of Bruce."[14]

Indeed, Governor Fuller was quite familiar with the Malden Court, since the Governor had been active in Malden politics, and, as with Judge Brooks, was a fiery Bull Mooser. Undoubtedly, Judge Bruce's tenure witnessed the litany of foibles associated with District Courts. Brief court sessions often in their entirety sometimes took a mere fifteen minutes. Arrogant judges' conduct was intemperate, cruel, and disrespectful. More pointedly, there was a blatant insensitivity to the fact that the District courts were the "people's courts" where "patience, humanity, and impartiality" surrendered to "rudeness" and "pomposity." When David I. Walsh was elected Governor in 1913, he lectured all of his judicial nominees regarding the importance of courtroom etiquette.[15] Walsh had personally been wounded by an inflated judicial self-importance, sustained by the use of mockery and ethnic degradation in the peoples' courts.

One could not expect those entrusted with law enforcement to respect the rights of a social or economic class or of citizens of a particular ethnic group when the presiding judge exhibited neither fairness, nor patience, nor humanity. Malden Jews suspected, however, that their courts exhibited but an inkling of the deeper, more pervasive prejudices adrift in the Massachusetts Commonwealth.

Chapter Seven

Real Americans

Detail of a young man from a family photograph

Kenneth Roberts served as the editor of the Malden High School yearbook in 1903 and he was an intelligent and popular student. After high school and Cornell University, and before he gained critical acclaim for his historical novels, including the monumental *Northwest Passage* (1937) and highly acclaimed *Arundel* (1930), he worked as a journalist. As a journalist he became an outspoken advocate for a halt to Jewish immigration to America especially in the 1920's when American concern for political reform retreated before a decade of nativism and reaction. In his writings of this time, Roberts articulated a political philosophy that was predicated upon racism and anti-Semitism.

Nowhere were Roberts' views more clearly evident than in his 1922 book entitled *Why Europe Leaves Home.*[1] This collection of post World War I reports were especially virulent, focusing upon Polish and Russian Jewry who sought refuge in America after World War I. Roberts' central theme was that Jews were undesirable immigrants for America. He characterized the Jews as human parasites who justified the debased treatment the East European world heaped upon them. Both in words and illustrations of this book, he portrayed Jews as justifiably despised, and thoroughly unassimilatable. Was America to become a land filled with Jews who could not and should not be allowed to mix with an already established population, fragmenting American society into a ghettoized land?

We can only speculate on Roberts' life in Malden, but it is fair to say that Roberts' anti-Semitism was nurtured in the city which introduced him to America's "Jewish" dilemma. Unlike Eliot Paul, Roberts was not especially concerned about reflecting upon his early Malden years, but Paul's observations about life in the city and the manifestations of anti-Semitism there were echoed in the political and social values of Kenneth Roberts. Clearly, the Jews of Malden stoked a common fire in the breast of two sensitive, literary talents. These two individuals shared the belief that ambition, criminal behavior, societal degeneracy, and the notorious Jewish "acumen" were destroying a city and an America that they loved. In the writings of Roberts, in particular, one senses none of the ambiguity about the legitimacy of the Jewish presence in America, as one clearly does in the writings of Eliot Paul. To Roberts, Jewry would wreak an unmitigated disaster upon American civilization and must be stopped.

In 1924, Kenneth Roberts published a short book entitled, *Concentrated New England: a Sketch of Calvin Coolidge*.[2] However, Roberts' book was a great deal more than a glittering portrait of the writer's favorite politician. For, in fact, the basis of Roberts' adulation revolved about Coolidge as an ethnic and racial symbol. To Roberts, Coolidge was the personification of a racially pure people amid the pristine New England landscape. Indeed, Coolidge was the kind of man that Roberts identified with America and, especially, Malden's early years.

Coolidge appreciated Malden's wooded glens and hillsides, and would have relished surveying Malden's bogs and marshlands.[3] To Roberts, Coolidge represented an earlier America, too, at least in myth: a time when the problems of race and ethnic complexity did not relegate Anglo-Saxonism to but one of many of America's intellectual and ancestral legacies. Coolidge was

> in appearance, in speech, and in outlook . . . a concentrated essence of the old bucolic New England — the New England farms and small towns and nasal twangs and long hours of work and horsehair sofas and reticence and church bells and straight thinking.[4]

But most of all, Roberts believed that Coolidge represented white Anglo-Saxon people who understood America and American values in ways that the Jews (and the Irish, too) could never appreciate. He was the hero of all those who wished to deny the spectre of cultural pluralism.

"Calvin Coolidge is the first president of the United States to have in his veins the blood of the original Americans," Roberts noted.[5] By this, Roberts meant that there was evidence that Coolidge may have even had American-Indian blood in his background, which further distinguished his Yankee roots and the propriety of being a "real American." In truth, Coolidge was a political and cultural idealogue who patronized America through a bizarre mixture of Puritan silence and work, which he valued, clearly, above the call of a needy humanity. He flaunted a cultural arrogance, that was heedless to the history of suffering and striving of America's newest immigrants.

Coolidge projected coldness and an insensitivity to those who labored and to those who wanted to familiarize America to their far away lands, and more importantly, deep felt dreams. To Malden's Jews, Coolidge did not possess the dignity, *hochem* or wisdom of reform-minded Republicanism. While Coolidge appealed to

Roberts and others who sought almost mythic hope in a provincial ideology, ethnic people reassessed the political landscape. Given the choice between Coolidge's demand for ideological conformity or their own historical commitment to the politics of discernment, Malden's Jews, and other American ethnics, increasingly maintained an open line to the Democratic Party and political humanism.

Malden Jewry voted against Coolidge in his two gubernatorial campaigns; but he was begrudgingly given a long withheld endorsement in his presidential bid in 1924. Yet, Coolidge fell some 22 percentage points below that of his predecessor, President Warren Harding, a known anti-Semite! Characteristically, Coolidge's rhetoric of 1919 captured his personal and social philosophy that may have endeared him to American nativists, but waxed hollow to Malden's Jews. When Coolidge stated, "there is no right to strike against the public safety by anybody, anywhere, anytime," it served to exacerbate the class differences in American society that Ward 7 recognized as a struggle involving them.

Jews in Malden were convinced that this brand of ideological provincialism would be deaf to their quest for the rights of full citizenship. Their religion and their determination to take full part in their new society were signposts to a host of individuals and forces that sought to trample Jewish rights. Since Coolidge was no advocate for an America based on cultural pluralism, his sanctimonious reverence for American values and the public welfare was a hollow promise and a mockery to the Jewish condition.

Lower class ethnics were obscure reformers, but their votes reveal their message. Coolidge and Draper had written ethnics off long before Al Smith won their votes. That a Jew must be a Jew demanded faith as well as wisdom; as such, a respect for people's differences possessed a most profound logic that Jewry could not ignore. Thus, parochial Republicanism helped assemble the Democratic Party's coalition of 1928 and, pivotally, in 1932.

In truth, Jews had difficulty identifying with the Democratic Party especially in Massachusetts, but they became convinced that in terms of social class, a Jewish-Irish relationship possessed a unique affinity. Coolidge's brand of Republicanism, as with that of Governor Draper, was predicated not on Republican reform, but on a philosophy of social and intellectual deference that was quite unacceptable to diverse ethnic pride and enormous ethnic sensitivity. As a case in point, the collective efforts of the Irish-led Boston Police Department in 1919 were viewed by Coolidge as an intellectually alien solution to a political problem in Massachusetts. American democracy, according to the ideologically provincal, had no place for alternative thinking, according to the Coolidge dictum. Jews simply could not identify with such a political personage, or be linked to such a political culture.

On the eve of the 1928 presidential election, a great debate was held by Malden's Deliberative Society. "Was it appropriate to view religion as a suitable election criteria," was the question to be resolved. That evening Raphael Boruchoff was forced to turn his back on his fellow Republicans who argued on behalf of the proposition and who were worried by the Catholicism of Al Smith. With sadness but unalterable determination to speak for human equity and truth, Boruchoff rejected any religious test for a political candidate. He rejected, indeed, any ethnic or ideological movement that somehow validated one person's Americanism at the expense of anothers. To Boruchoff, the Republican Party had lost its way, despite the rousing victory that the Republican Party enjoyed in the election of 1928. In droves, Malden Jewry and other ethnics throughout America voted for Smith, taking a stand that would foreshadow later political changes.

Italian Immigrants

...in Malden, c. 1925

In the election of 1932, the *Malden News* ran a front page editorial urging the reelection of President Hoover. Malden's population at that time had grown beyond sixty-five percent ethnic with Jews and the Irish comprising some fifty percent of the vote and the emerging Italian population mushrooming to nearly fifteen percent of Malden's voters. Indeed, the tides of ethnic population had altered the city.

Clearly, the ethnic vote could not be ignored, and the volatile but heavy Jewish turnout now required a degree of courting. The *Malden News* pleaded the following argument. "We believe that a generation from now when Hoover is viewed in the light of history that no descendant of men or women who vote against him tomorrow will point to it with any degree of pride."[6] Ironically, Calvin Coolidge went on national radio the evening of November 7, 1932 to plead the case for the Republican Party.

Over thirty years of electoral returns, however, demonstrate that the Malden Irish vote was expectantly Democratic and the Jewish vote was frequently Republican, but the relationship between Irish and Jewish electoral trends illuminate more fundamental political considerations affecting ethnics and the growth of Massachusetts' political culture. What remains implicit in their collective voting history is the reality that questions of human equity and aspirations of social class superseded all other political considerations and, in fact, would remain a prime component of ethnic political consciousness.

The fact that reform minded Republicanism had appealed to Jewish sensibilities and economic aspirations were significantly eroded, ultimately, by an often arrogant ideology that chastized Massachusetts people because of alleged deficiencies from everything from respect of the free enterprize system, to the ardor of their patriotism, and even their fundamental human values. Jews grew alienated by an ideology that shunned cultural and political differences, and which inferred that *their legitimacy* as Americans was not beyond being questioned. To the Jew, America was not just a place, but an historic ideal that denied any such assumption.

For the Jews, those first few decades of the twentieth century suggested a number of observations about Malden, if not America. First, the periods of ethnic antagonism between Yankees and Irish were fierce and unrelenting. The economic subordination of the Irish became a painful, incessant sore upon Irish-American conciousness. As such, Irish-Democratic politics were practiced as a "magnificent obsession."

For the most part, Yankee Malden did little to temper this strife or promote any form of ecumenical harmony. Malden's wealthiest citizens and business firms were often benefactors and philanthropists of some note, but Malden's Irish and other ethnics within the city were never the recipients of their largess.

This intense ethnic hostility affected Jews, too. The Riot of 1911 demonstrated that acts of violence and physical intimidation were inspired by prejudice and antipathy, despite the absence of any intra-city rationale for social conflict. Irish and Jews shared little in the way of turf and barely competed or communicated with one another in any meaningful aspect of their shared Malden existence. No other similar violence occurred within the city, although doubtless Jewish and Irish youths were known to exchange taunts and barbs. In time, too, the police force became less concerned about rotating its Suffolk Square police officers, and the Irish police and Jewish citizenry often became well-acquainted.

But the Jewish population never got over a degree of outrage directed at those "progressive forces" who deprived them of equal protection under the law or other aspects of their full citizenship.

The anti-Semitism of Malden officialdom was, however, more than only dismaying. Jews began to suspect that just as the Irish were held in a kind of economic restraint, Jews, too were restrained but by a manipulative and somewhat conspiratorial tenor to Malden life.

Jews became suspicious of the "progressive *shtik*" they witnessed. How could the call for social and political reform be compatible with the arbitrary enforcement of law, with a capricious selection of juries, and all too often insensitive rendering of both political and judicial judgements? Might it be that Irish and Jewish animosities were but a convenient foil for distracting ethnic cooperation and coalition building? Was the progressive call for "American virtue" a mere ruse in the quest for social control of disparate cultures and peoples?

Through public remonstrances and a discerning voting record, the local Jews made their presence felt in an important way. The message which emanated from the Jewish community was, in fact, that American *pluralism* was uncompromisable. A commitment to American pluralism became the cutting edge of a fundamental political and philosophical test that sustained the fact that a minority people could maintain their given identity, however insular or assimilationist, and contribute to the historic American mission. Unswervingly, this was American-Jewry's fateful commitment, and it was rooted in the first generation Jew's voting record and social philosophy.

For almost two decades Jews continued to protest their exclusion from serving on Middlesex juries, but they generally ignored being shunned from particular neighborhoods in the city. They were not interested in moving to where they were not wanted, but they tenaciously rejected any political party or governmental unit that attempted to prevent them from *being* what they wanted.

Within the city, especially during the decade of the 1920's, first generation Jewish-Americans witnessed additional affronts to their citizenship and their Jewish identity. When a donation of the infamous anti-Semitic tract, *The Protocols of the Elders of Zion*, was made to the Malden Public Library, it enjoyed a most vigorous circulation despite Jewish protest. In fact, it took years of protests before the library agreed to remove the book from its circulation file.

Also in the early twenties, a branch of the Ku Klux Klan operated in Malden's Maplewood neighborhood, just on the edge of Linden. Clearly, it was the economic energy of Malden's Jewish community that fueled Malden's Klan, since those individuals associated with the Klan would later be part of the city's Nazi Bund movement in the early nineteen thirties.

Organizations predicated upon hate and anti-Semitism took root in Malden, and elsewhere in America. But Malden's Jewish citizens continued to vote with a discerning eye, helped sustain an historic political coalition centered in the Irish led Democratic party, and, in their convictions, held true to a profound commitment in the Jewish-American experience.

Sons and daughters of the first immigrants, 1932

Introduction

1. J. Joseph Huthmacher, *Massachusetts People and Politics, 1919-1933* (Originally published by Belknap Press, Harvard University, 1959; reprint by Atheneum, New York, 1969), Chapter One.
2. Ibid. See also Huthmacher's article, "Charles E. Hughes and Charles F. Murphy: "The Metamorphosis of Progressivism," *New York History* (January, 1965), 25-40.
3. Among the more important monographs dealing with the relationship between Progressivism and Protestantism are in the following: George Mowry, *The California Progressives* (1951) as well as his *The Era of Theodore Roosevelt, 1900-1912* (1958); Henry May, *The End of American Innocence* (1959); Richard Hofstadter, *The Age of Reform: From Bryan to F.D.R.* (1955). See the essay of Alfred D. Morison, ed., *The Letters of Theodore Roosevelt*, Vol 8, pp. 1462-65. A more recent study attesting to the Progressive and Protestant relationship is Robert Crunden's *Ministers of Reform: The Progressives' Achievements in American Civilization, 1889-1920* (1982).
4. An exception to this trend has been the work of John D. Buenker. See his *Urban Liberalism and Progressive Reform* (1973). Oscar Handlin's *Race and Nationality in American Life* (1948) and *The American People in the Twentieth Century* (1954) consider the immigrant as being more concerned with survival than politics and tends to disregard the subject of ethnic political activity as, at best, low as an immigrant priority. Huthmacher's article, "Urban Liberalism and the Age of Reform," *Mississippi Valley Historical Review*, 49 (September, 1962), 231-41, remains the author's most direct statement regarding ethnic political contributions during the period. See also Arthur Mann's *Yankee Reformers in an Urban Age* (1954).
5. Robert Crunden, *Ministers of Reform*. Crunden credits Brandeis as a progressive but, generally, believes that Jews and other ethnics did not play a significant role in promoting the movement. For the most part, however, Crunden's book focuses upon prominent Americans, especially in the arts. As such, Crunden's political observations are quite dependent on traditional scholarship.

6. Malden's most prominent historian was Deloraine Pendre Corey. See his *The History of Malden, Massachusetts, 1633-1785* (Malden, 1899). Also see Samuel Adams Drake, *History of Middlesex County*, 2 vols. (Boston, 1880).

7. The local polling records have been analyzed for the period 1900-1932 in conjunction with the city's voting records. The polling records contain data regarding residency, occupation, and age. See the *Poll Books, City of Malden, 1900-1932* (Malden City Hall, Assessors Office Archives). Voting returns have been culled from the local press as well as the city's official records. See *Records of the Mayor and Alderman, 1900-1932* (Malden City Hall, Archives of the Office of the Clerk). Huthmacher noted that the Malden Irish and the Jews of Malden were important ethnic constituencies, but he failed to explore either group in any thorough sense.

8. Claudia Bushman, *"A Good Poor Man's Wife:" Being a Chronicle of Harriet Hanson Robinson and Her Family in Nineteenth Century New England* (Hanover, New Hampshire: University Press of New England, 1981) p. 93 and pp. 210-11. For a fine example of social and cultural change affecting Malden, see the following: *Memorial of the Celebration of the Two Hundred and Fiftieth Anniversary of the Incorporation of the Town of Malden, Massachusetts, May, 1899* (Cambridge, The University Press, 1900), and especially the "Address of Welcome" by Deloraine Pendre Corey, President of the Day, p. 199.

9. Joel Perlmann, "Beyond New York: The Occupations of Russian Jewish Immigrants in Providence, R.I. and in Other Small Jewish Communities," *American Jewish History* Vol. LXXII, No. 3, (March, 1983), 369-394.

10. The distinguished work of Irving Howe, *World of Our Fathers: The Journey of the East European Jews to America and the Life They Found and Made* (New York: Touchstone, 1976) recognized that his book was primarily concerned with New York Jews. "Let us now praise obscure men" (p. 646) was a salute to the resurrection of an even larger immigrant legacy which any single work could not encompass. However, Thomas Kessner's study of occupational patterns among Jews and Italians in New York City seemed to suggest that Jews experienced a change in occupational status within a single generation, with a significant percentage of manual workers moving along to a white collar occupational status. See his *The Golden Door: Italian and Jewish Immigrant Mobility in New York City 1800-1915* (New York: 1977), p. 60. Malden's Jewish community possessed an occupational profile that was decidely white collar, if lower white collar. In fact, a comparison of the city's Jews

occupational pattern to that of the local Irish occupational pattern demonstrates a marked difference in occupational direction. Manual labor all but dominates the Irish economic profile, while small scale entrepreneurship characterize the Jewish ward. Irving Howe's *World of Our Fathers* examines many of these concerns.

Notes and References

Chapter One

1. Eliot Paul, *Linden on the Saugus Branch* (New York: Random House, 1947), Ch. 1. Many of Paul's earliest novels comment upon New England life than in and about cities such as Malden. See the following novels: *Indelible: A Story of Life, Love, and Music in Five Movements* (Boston: Houghton Miflin Company, 1922); *Impromptu: A Novel in Four Movements* (New York: Alfred A. Knopf, 1923); *Imperturbe: A Novel of Peace without Victory* (New York: Alfred A. Knopf, 1924); *The Governor of Massachusetts: A Novel in Three Parts* (New York: Horace Liveright, 1930).
2. Paul, *Linden on The Saugus Branch*, p. 4.
3. *Ibid.,* p. 26-27.
4. *Ibid.,* p. 5.
5. *Ibid.,* p. 104.
6. *Ibid.*
7. *Ibid.,* p. 69.
8. *Malden City Press*, October, 8, 1881, p. 1.
9. Paul, *Linden on The Saugus Branch*, pp. 282-285.
10. *Ibid.,* p. 263.
11. *Ibid.*
12. Eliot Paul, *Impromptu: A Novel in Four Movements*, pp. 5-6.
13. Paul, *Linden on The Saugus Branch*, p. 252.
14. *Ibid.,* p. 263.
15. *The Edgeworth Advocate*, October 7, 1907, p. 1.
16. See the *Malden Evening News*, August 10, 1908, "Edgeworth Hebrew Association," p. 1; in addition, see the *Malden Mail*, August 10, 1908, p. 3.
17. Bill Mini, "Looking Back . . . Old Suffolk Square," *Suffolk Square Reunion Society*, November 27, 1982.
18. *Malden Mail*, August 19, 1904, p. 1.
19. Poll Books, 1900-1932, City of Malden, Archives of the Assessor. The following data is based on representative samples for the years 1900, 1904, 1908, 1912, 1916, 1920, 1924, 1928 and 1932. In fact, each of the years from 1900-1932 were examined, but for purposes of the sample four year intervals were utilized in the analysis. Jewish Ward 7 and Irish Ward 2 were

scrutinized for the following: ethnic composition, occupation characteristics, age, and geographical movement within each ward.

20. *Malden Mail*, August 25, 1905, p. 2.
21. Interview with Mildred Boruchoff Goldish, July 21, 1984.
22. *Malden Mail*, April 1, 1907, p. 2; also, *Malden Mail*, October 24, 1910, p. 2.
23. *Malden Evening News*, November 15, 1915, p. 8.
24. *Malden Evening News*, November 26, 1915, p. 1.
25. Louis Schmier, "For Him the 'Schwartzers' Couldn't Do Enough: A Jewish Peddler and His Black Customers Look at Each Other," *American Jewish Historical Quarterly* Vol. LXXIII, No. 1 (September, 1983) 39-55.

Notes and References

Chapter Two

1. See Lawrence H. Fuchs, *The Political Behavior of American Jews* (Glencoe, Illinois, The Free Press) p. 137 and p. 58; David Burner, *The Politics of Provincialism: The Democratic Party in Transition, 1918-1932* (New York, Alfred A. Knopf, 1968); Joseph Dorinson, "Jewish Politics: The Art of Survival" in *America's Ethnic Politics*, edited by Joseph S. Roucek and Bernard Eisenberg (Westport, Connecticut, Greenwood Press, 1982) pp. 237-38; Nathaniel Weyl, *Jews in American Politics* (New Rochelle, N.Y., Arlington House in 1968); Richard M. Abrams, *Conservatism in a Progressive Era, Massachusetts 1900-1912* (Cambridge, Harvard University Press, 1964) remains the most reliable assessment of early Massachusetts voting direction despite its absence of quantitative evidence.

2. See Professor Ralph Janis' use of the term "ministate" in his review of Olivier Zunz's *The Changing Face of Inequality: Urbanization, Industrial Development, and Immigrants in Detroit, 1880-1920* published in *The American Historical Review* Vol. 88, No. 4 (October, 1983), p. 1088.

3. All of the voting data presented here and throughout the study was taken from the *Records of The Mayor and Aldermen*, Office of the Clerk's Archives, City of Malden, for the period 1900-1932. In addition, the local press was used for voter breakdowns according to precincts when the official record did not do so.

4. Lawrence Fuchs, *The Political Behavior of American Jews*, p. 60; Melvin Urofsky, *Louis Brandeis and The Progressive Tradition* (Boston: Little Brown, 1981), Ch. 4.

5. See Figures 5 and 6.

6. *Address of His Excellency David I. Walsh to the Two Branches of The Legislature of Massachusetts*, January 8, 1914 (Boston: Wright and Potter Printing Company, 1914).

7. *Ibid.*, p. 66.

8. For a far different appraisal of Walsh, see Dorothy G. Wayman, *David I. Walsh, Citizen-Patriot* (Milwaukee: Bruce Publishing Company, 1952) as well as J.J. Huthmacher, *Massachusetts People and Politics, 1919-1933*.

9. See Samuel Walker McCall, *Patriotism of the American Jew* (New York: Plymouth Press, Inc., 1924).

131

10. *Ibid.*, p. 249.

11. *Records of The Deliberative Assembly, 1897-1907,* and *1908-1923,* Malden Public Library, Archives. In addition see Albert Ammon's *Scrapbook on The Malden Deliberative Society,* Malden Public Library, Archives. The local press covered the proceedings of the Society in great detail. For example, see the *Malden Evening News,* March 8, 1897, p. 1 for a discussion of "The Restriction of Immigration."

12. Interview with Mildred Boruchoff Goldish, July 21, 1984.

13. *Ibid.*

Chapter Three

1. W.H. Winship, *Malden Industries, 1640-1951* (typed manuscript, Malden Public Library, Archives). Winshop's study provides both an inventory of Malden's firms as well as an indication of the industrial cycles experienced by the city.

2. R.H. Lord, *History of the Archdiocese of Boston*, Volume III, 1866-1943 (New York: Sheed and Ward, 1944), pp. 280-282.

3. *Malden City Press*, "Edgeworth Tannery: A Historical Sketch," January 14, 1882, p. 1.

4. Lord, *History of The Archdiocese of Boston*, Vol. 3, pp. 280-282. See the *Malden News* for other articles relating to economic dislocation within the ward: August 8, 1893, p. 4 and September 19, 1895, p. 4.

5. Richard Hofstadter, *The Age of Reform: From Bryan to FDR* (New York: Alfred A. Knopf, 1972), p. 168.

6. William V. Shannon, *The American Irish* (New York: Macmillan, 1963), p. 200.

7. A variety of local business reports are on file in the Malden Public Library, Permanent Local Collection.

8. See Margery W. Davies, *Women's Place Is at The Typewriter: Office Work and Office-Workers* (Philadelphia, Temple University Press, 1982) for a thorough analysis of this idea.

9. Claudia Bushman, "A Good Poor Man's Wife," p. 119.

10. *Ibid.*, pp. 110-111.

11. *Malden Police Records, 1900-1932* (Malden Police Archives, Malden, Massachusetts) reveal the names and addresses of its police officers.

Notes and References

Chapter Four

1. Abrams, *Conservatism in a Progressive Era*, p. 133.
2. Alec Barbrook, *God Save the Commonwealth: An Electoral History of Massachusetts* (Amherst, University of Massachusetts Press, 1973) p. 16.
3. *The Jewish Advocate*, October 6, 1911, p. 8.
4. The Malden Democratic City Committee has been well charted by the newspaper files of the Malden Public Library, beginning from 1886 through 1932. Irish dominance of the party in the community was evidenced in these newspaper reports.
5. See the *Malden Evening News*, November 6, 1928, p. 1.
6. *Ibid.*
7. *Malden News*, March 16, 1916, "Deliberative Debate on Encouraging New Industries for Malden," p. 1.
8. *Malden Mail*, August 19, 1904, p. 1. See the early works of Malden native, Eliot Paul, including *Indelible: A Story of Life, Love, and Music in Five Movements* (Boston, Houghton Mifflin Company, 1922); *Impromptu: A Novel in Four Movements* (New York, Alfred A. Knopf, 1923); *Imperturbe: A Novel of Peace without Victory* (New York, Alfred A. Knopf, 1924); perhaps Paul's most direct allusions to the growth of Malden Jewry appear in his remembrance of his early life in Malden, entitled *Linden on the Saugus Line*. Kenneth Roberts' bitterly anti-Semitic book, *Why Europe Leaves Home*, reveals that the Malden nurtured writer came to question the place of the East European Jew in America.
9. Gordon L. Geller, "Jewish Life in Boston As Reflected in the Boston Jewish Advocate, 1905-1910," typed manuscript, (May, 1965, American Jewish Archives) 6-7.
10. See the works of Eliot Paul already cited. In addition, the early works of Kenneth Roberts also sustains the change of intellectual anti-Semitism, particularly *Why Europe Leaves Home*, pp. 99-120.
11. See the *Revised Ordinances and Charters of the City of Malden* (1939, Malden City Archives, Assessors Office, Malden City Hall), Appendix, Table Showing Population, Valuation and Rate of Taxation Per $1000, Since Malden Became A City; in addition see W.H. Winship, *Malden Industries, 1640-1951* (manuscript in the Malden Public Library, Archives.

The Malden Public Library also contains an historical section devoted to Malden City Directories that detail the economic vibrancy of Jewish life within the larger city.

12. Richard Klayman, "The Boycott of Malden's Jews: The Summer of 1912," in *The Malden Evening News*, August 9, 1982. See also J. Jacob Nensner, *The Rise of the Jewish Community of Boston, 1880-1914* (B.A. Thesis, Harvard University, 1953) 131-134.

13. Richard Hofstadter, *The Age of Reform*, p. 172.

Chapter Five

1. Lawrence Fuchs, *The Political Behavior of American Jews*, pp. 51-52.
2. *Malden News*, September 14, 1912, p. 1.
3. *Ibid.*
4. Voting data was gathered from the *Records of the Mayor and Alderman, 1900-1932*, Malden City Archives, City Clerks Office, Malden City Hall; in addition, the local press accounts of electoral returns was consulted for the entire period to both corroborate the official returns and, occassionally, fill in data missing from the city's official records. The following graphs are based on the collected data which is in my possession.
5. For the most part, assessments of the Jewish vote have been gauged by a focus on pivotal elections, usually taken to be the 1928 Presidential election, the 1932 or 1936 Presidential contests, and some specific elections of an earlier day. For example, Lawrence H. Fuchs, *The Political Behavior of American Jews* (Glencoe, Illinois: Free Press, 1956) suggests that the election of Woodrow Wilson in 1912 was pivotal in the establishment of Jewish political ties, based on the Jewish vote in New York and Boston. (p. 60). Malden's results in 1912 suggest a different conclusion as to the significance of the 1912 contest, as well as an overall difference as to the Jewish electoral pattern. Malden's Jewish vote gravitated less toward party affiliation and more toward the politics of political reform. David Burner's *The Politics of Provincialism* suggests a vacillation to the Jewish vote until the 1928 election, but no more significant conclusion can be rendered from his 1916-1932 sample (see p. 241). Small city's Jewry voted from what has been characterized as an historic sense of liberalism, but also because of specific problems that the local Jewish community experienced. In addition see Michael S. Kramer and Mark R. Levy, *The Ethnic Factor: How America's Minorities Decide Elections* (New York: Simon and Shuster, 1972) pp. 100-102; Edgar Litt, *The Political Cultures of Massachusetts* and Litt's *Beyond Pluralism: Ethnic Politics in America* (Glenview, Illinois, Scott, Foreman, 1970).
6. See Harold U. Faulkner, "Eben S. Draper," *Dictionary of American Biography*, (1930) 435; also, Alec Barbrook, *God Save The Commonwealth*, p. 26; Richard Abrams, *Conservatism in a Progressive*

Era, pp. 187-189; Albert Bushnell Hart, *Commonwealth History of Massachusetts*, Vol. 5, (New York, The States History Company, 1930) pp. 63, 177, 178, 180; for a sympathetic appraisal of the Draper years see William Andrew Murphy, *The Administrations of Hon. Eben Sumner Draper* (Boston, Privately Printed, 1911).

7. See Abrams and Barbrook in the above citations.

8. Ibid. See also Philippa Strum, *Louis D. Brandeis: Justice for The People* (Cambridge: Harvard University Press, 1984), especially p. 84.

9. Abrams, *Convervatism a Progressive Era*, Chapter Eight; also see Melvin Urofsky, *Louis Brandeis and the Progressive Tradition* (Boston, Little, Brown and Company, 1981) pp. 41-46.

10. Moses Rischin, *The Promised City: New York's Jews, 1870-1914* (Cambridge, Massachusetts, Harvard University Press, 1962) pp. 90-91; Nathan M. Kaganoff's article, "An Orthodox Rabbinate in the South: Tobias Geffen, 1870-1970," *American Jewish Historical Quarterly* Vol. LXXIII, No. 1 (September, 1983) 66-67 alludes to the potentially high percentage of Jews incarcerated for crimes in Pittsburg and Atlanta; see also Jenna Weissman Joselit, *Our Gang: Jewish Crime and the New York Jewish Community, 1900-1940*; the historical analysis of crime has gained scholarly attention in recent years, see especially the work of Eric Monkkonen, *Police in Urban America, 1860-1920* (Cambridge, Eng.; New York: Cambridge University Press, 1981), Chapter 2, "Arrest Trends, 1860-1920."

11. Graphs charting Jewish crime in Malden were based on collected data of the *Malden Police Arrest Books*, 1900-1932.

12. See the *Poll Books, 1900-1932, City of Malden* and the city directories for the period. In addition, Malden's first rabbi, Ber Boruchoff, kept rather detailed marriage records in which he recorded the following data from 1905-1939: name of the newlyweds, age, occupation, place of birth, first marriage or not, parents name for both individuals, and date issued for the marriage license date joined in marriage. The composite portrait of the Jewish community which emerges from these records demonstrates the entrepreneurial nature of the Malden community. See the *Notebooks of Ber Boruchoff*, American Jewish Historical Society, Waltham, Massachusetts.

13. *Malden News*, February 2, 1914, p. 2; *Malden News*, October 31, 1914, p. 1; *Malden News*, May 28, 1915, p. 7. The reporter in the October 31, 1914, article observed that "Attorneys of note say that many of the laws about Sunday opening are unconstitutional, but the new order to enforce them effects only poor storekeepers who are not able to contest. The Suffolk

Square section is the hardest hit." In fact, as the arrest records demonstrate, Jews were singled out for violation of the Sunday closing ordinances, notwithstanding the allowance of Jewish owned businesses closed on Saturday to remain open on Sunday from 6 A.M. until 10 A.M.

Chapter Six

1. The jury lists were published in the Malden newspaper from 1900-1932. No resident of Ward 7 with a Jewish surname or corresponding address that might identify them as residing in the Jewish neighborhood was found until 1933. See *Malden News*, August 15, 1933, p. 3.
2. *Malden News*, July 13, 1912, p. 1. See also *Malden News*, September 4, 1912, p. 1.
3. *Malden News*, March 9, 1923, p. 1.
4. *Report of the Judicature Commission*, January, 1920, printed in the *Massachusetts Law Quarterly*; in addition, see the "Second and Final Report on the Judicature Commission, 1921" *Massachusetts Law Quarterly*, Vol. 6, No. 2, Special Number (January, 1921).
5. *Ibid.*
6. Albert B. Hart, *Commonwealth History of Massachusetts*, Vol. 5 (New York: The States History Company, 1930) p. 102.
7. *Ibid.*
8. *Malden News*, July 24, 1911, p. 1; July 26, 1911, p. 1; July 27, 1911, p. 1, August 2, 1911, p. 1; August 9, 1911, p. 1.
9. *Ibid.*
10. *Malden News*, July 27, 1911, p. 1.
11. *Ibid.*
12. Lawrence Carter, compiler, *The Memoirs of Lawrence Graham Brooks* (Boston: privately printed, 1981) p. 268.
13. *Ibid.*
14. *Ibid.*
15. Dorothy G. Wayman, *David I. Walsh*, Ch. 5 and 6.
16. In 1933 the B'nai Brith sent a copy of the *'Protocols of the Wise Men of Zion' A Spurious and Fraudulent Document* by Sigmund Livingston. This document was placed in the inside flap of the *Protocols* text, and both were removed from circulation.

Notes and References

Chapter Seven

1. Kenneth Roberts, *Why Europe Leaves Home* (Indianapolis: The Bobbs-Merrill Company, 1920).
2. Kenneth Roberts, *Concentrated New England: A Sketch of Calvin Coolidge* (Indianapolis: The Bobbs-Merrill Company, 1924) p. 8.
3. William Allen White, *A Puritan in Babylon* (New York: Macmillan, 1938) pp. 41-42.
4. Kenneth Roberts, *A Sketch of Calvin Coolidge*, p. 8.
5. *Ibid.*, p. 5.
6. *Malden Evening News*, November 7, 1932, p. 1.

Bibliography

Primary Sources

Directories
Malden City Directories, 1900, 1902, 1904, 1906, 1908, 1909-1933.
Malden Public Library, Permanent Collection.
W.H. Winshop, *Malden Industries, 1640-1951*, typed manuscript.
Malden Public Library, Archives.

Journals
H.W. Fison Papers, 1912-1942. Malden Public Library, Archives.
Records of the Deliberative Assembly, 1875-1879, 1888-1896, 1897-1907, 1908-1923. Malden Public Library, Archives.
The Register of the Malden Historical Society, Malden, Massachusetts, Number 1-6, 1910-1920 (Lynn, Massachusetts, Frank S. Whitten, Printer, 1920).

Newspapers
Boston Mirror
Bunker Hill Aurora
Malden City Press
Malden Evening News
Malden Free Press
Malden Mail
Malden Messinger
Malden Mirror
The Edgeworth Advocate
The Jewish Advocate
The Jewish Voice

Maps
Atlas of the City of Malden, Middlesex County, Massachusetts 1897.
(Published by George H. Walker, Boston)

Memoirs

Rabbi Ber Boruchoff, Notebooks, American Jewish Historical Society, Waltham, Massachusetts.

Lawrence Carter, compiler. *The Memoirs of Lawrence Graham Brooks*. Privately printed. Boston, 1981.

Ruth L.S. Child, *History of the Schools of Malden, 1649-1939*, typed manuscript. Malden Public Library, Archives.

Public Records

Arrest Records of the Malden Police Department, 1900-1932. Malden, Massachusetts Police Department, Archives, Malden, Massachusetts.

Malden Court Ledgers, 1900-1940, Malden Court House, Archives, Malden, Massachusetts.

Poll Books of the City of Malden, 1900-1932. Office of the Assessor, Archives, Malden, Massachusetts.

Records of the Mayor and Aldermen, 1900-1932. Office of the Clerk Archives, Malden, Massachusetts.

Revised Ordinances and Charters of the City of Malden 1939, Office of the Assessor, Archives, Malden, Massachusetts.

Scrapbooks/Photographic Collections

Albert Amman, Malden Deliberative Assembly, Malden Public Library, Archives, Malden, Massachusetts.

Bernard Kaufman, Historic Postcard Collection of Malden, Massachusetts, privately owned.

City of Malden, Engineering Department, Photographic Archives, Malden, Massachusetts.

Elsie G. Goodman, Photographic Collection of Suffolk Square, privately owned.

F.E. Rea, compiler, Malden Auditorium, Malden Public Library, Archives, Malden, Massachusetts.

Malden Public Library Scrapbook, Malden Public Library, Archives, Malden, Massachusetts.

Notes on the History of Boston Jewry, 1880-1914, Miscellaneous Files, American Jewish Archives, Cincinnati, Ohio.

Secondary Sources

Books

Abrams, Richard M. *Conservatism in a Progressive Era, Massachusetts Politics 1900-1912.* Cambridge: Harvard University Press, 1964.

Ainsley, Lesley G. *Boston Mahatma: Martin Lomasney.* Boston: Bruce Humphreys, 1949.

Anderson, Kristi. *The Creation of a Democratic Majority, 1928-1936.* Chicago: The University of Chicago Press, 1979.

Archdeacon, Thomas J. *Becoming American: An Ethnic History.* New York: The Free Press, 1983.

Bailey, Harry and Katz, Ellis. *Ethnic Group Politics.* Columbus, Ohio: Charles E. Merrill, 1964.

Barbrook, Alec. *God Save the Commonwealth: An Electoral History of Massachusetts.* Amherst: University of Massachusetts Press, 1973.

Berger, David. ed. *The Legacy of Jewish Migration: 1881 and Its Impact.* New York: Brooklyn College Press, 1983.

Brown, Richard D. *Massachusetts: A Bicentennial History.* New York: W.W. Norton and Co., Inc., 1978.

Buenker, John D. *Urban Liberalism and Progressive Reform,* New York: Scribner, 1973.

Buenker, John D. *Immigration and Ethnicity: A Guide to Information Sources.* Detroit: Gale Research Co., 1977.

Buenker, John D. *Progressive Reform: A Guide to Information Sources.* Detroit: Gale Research Co., 1980.

Burner, David. *The Politics of Provincialism: The Democratic Party in Transition, 1918-1932.* New York, Alfred A. Knopf, 1968.

Burnham, Walter Dean. *Critical Elections and the Mainsprings of American Politics.* New York: W.W. Norton, 1970.

Buchman, Claudia L. *"A Good Poor Man's Wife:" Being a Chronicle of Harriet Hanson Robinson and Her Family in Nineteenth Century New England.* Hanover, New Hampshire: University Press of New England, 1981.

Carpenter, Niles. *Immigrants and their Children.* Washington, D.C., Govt. Printing Office, 1927.

Clark, Dennis. *The Irish Relations: Trials of an Immigrant Tradition.* East Brunswick, N.J.: Associated University Presses, Inc., 1982.

Coben, Stanley and Ratner. Norman, eds. *The Development of an American Culture.* New York: St. Martins Press, 2nd ed., 1983.

Coolidge, Calvin. *Have Faith in Massachusetts: A Collection of Speeches and Messages.* Boston: Houghton, Mifflin Company, 1919.

Commons, John R. *Races and Immigrants in America.* New York: The MacMillan Company, 1930 (1st edn., 1927).

Corey, Deloraine Pendre. *The History of Malden, Massachusetts, 1633-1785.* Malden, Massachusetts: 1899.

Cox, Edward Franklin. *State and National Voting in Federal Elections, 1910-1970.* Hamden, Connecticut: Archon Books, 1972.

Crunden, Robert M. *Ministers of Reform: The Progressives' Achievement in American Civilization, 1889-1920.* New York: Basic Books, Inc., 1982.

Curley, James Michael. *I'd Do It Again! A Record of All My Uproarious Years.* Englewood Cliffs, New Jersey: Prentice-Hall, Inc., 1957.

Currar, Thomas J. *Xenophobia and Immigration, 1820-1930.* Boston: Twayne Publishers, 1975.

Dana, Herma. *The Early Days of the Beth Israel Hospital, 1911-1920.* Privately printed: May, 1950.

Davies, Margery W. *Women's Place Is at the Typewriter: Office Work and Office Workers, 1870-1930.* Philadelphia: Temple University Press, 1982.

Dineen, Joseph F. *The Purple Shamrock: The Hon. James Michael Curley of Boston.* New York: W.W. Norton & Company, 1949.

Divine, Robert A. *American Immigration Policies: A History.* Washington, D.C.: 1963.

Dubnow, Semen. *History of the Jews in Russia and Poland.* (English translation, I. Friedlander, 3 Vols. Philadelphia: The Jewish Publication Society of America, 1916-1920.

Fehrenbacher, Don E. *History and American Society: Essays of David M. Potter.* New York: Oxford University Press, 1973.

Feingold, Henry L. *A Midrash on American Jewish History.* Albany: State University of New York Press, 1982.

Feingold, Henry L. *Zion in America: The Jewish Experience from Colonial Times to the Present.* New York: Twayne Publishers, Inc., 1974.

Feldstein, Stanley. *The Land that I Show You.* Garden City, New York: Anchor Press, 1978.

Fried, Albert. *The Rise and Fall of the Jewish Gangster.* New York: Holt, Rinehart and Winston, 1980.

Fuchs, Lawrence H. *The Political Behavior of American Jews.* Glencoe, Illinois: The Free Press, 1956.

Fuchs, Lawrence H. *American Ethnic Politics.* New York: Harper Torchbooks, 1968.

Garis, Roy L. *Immigration Restriction: A Study of the Opposition to the Regulation of Immigration into the United States.* New York: The MacMillan Company, 1927.

Ginsburg, Yona. *Jews in a Changing Neighborhood: A Study of Mattapan.* New York: Free Press, 1975.

Goldman, Ralph M. *Search for Consensus: The Story of the Democratic Party.* Philadelphia: Temple University Press, 1979.

Gordon, Milton M. *Assimilation in American Life.* New York: Oxford University Press, 1964.

Goren, Arthur. *New York Jews and the Quest for Community: The Kehillah Experiment, 1908-1922.* New York: Columbia University Press, 1970.

Greeley, Andrew M. *The Irish Americans and The Rise to Money and Power.* New York: Harper and Row, Publishers, 1981.

Gulick, Luther H. *The Evolution of the Budget in Massachusetts.* New York: The Macmillan Company, 1920.

Halpert, Stephen and Brenda. *Brahmins and Bullyboys: G. Frank Radway's Boston Album.* Boston: Houghton Mifflin Company, 1973.

Handlin, Oscar. *Adventure in Freedom: Three Hundred Years of Jewish Life in America.* New York: McGraw-Hill, 1954.

Handlin, Oscar. *Race and Nationality in American Life.* Boston: Little, Brown and Company, 1948.

Handlin, Oscar. *The American People in the Twentieth Century.* Cambridge: Harvard University Press, 1954.

Handlin, Oscar. *The Uprooted.* Boston: Little, Brown, 1973.

Hansen, Marcus L. *The Immigrant in American History.* Cambridge: Harvard University Press, 1940.

Hapgood, Hutchins. *The Spirit of the Ghetto.* Cambridge: The Belknap Press of Harvard University, 1967. (1st edn. 1902).

Hart, Albert Bushnell, ed. *Commonwealth History of Massachusetts.* 5 vols., New York: The States History Company, 1930.

Hartmann, Edward G. *The Movement to Americanize the Immigrant.* New York: Columbia University Press, 1948.

Hennessy, Michael E. *Four Decades of Massachusetts Politics, 1890-1935.* Norwood, Massachusetts: The Norwood Press, 1935.

Hennessy, Michael E. *Twenty-Five years of Massachusetts Politics, 1890-1915.* Boston: Practical Politics, Inc., 1917.

Higham, John. *Strangers in the Land: Patterns of American Nativism 1860-1925.* New Brunswick, N.J., Rutgers University Press, 1955.

Higham, John. *Send These to Me: Jews and Other Immigrants in Urban America.* New York: Athaneum, 1975).

Higham, John, ed. *Ethnic Leadership in America.* Baltimore: Johns Hopkin University Press, 1978.

Herlihy, Elisabeth M., ed. *Fifty Years of Boston.* Boston: 1932.

Hofstadter, Richard. *The Age of Reform: From Bryan to FDR.* New York: Alfred A. Knopf, 1972.

Hofstadter, Richard, ed. *The Progressive Movement: 1900-1915.* Englewood Cliffs: Prentice Hall, 1963.

Howe, Irving. *World of Our Fathers: The Journey of the East European Jews to America and the Life They Found and Made.* New York: Touchstone, 1976.

Howe, Irving and Libo, Kenneth. *How We Lived: A Documentary History of Immigrant Jews in America, 1880-1930.* New York: Richard Manak Publishers, 1979.

Hourwich, Isaac A. *Immigration and Labor.* New York: G.P. Putnam's Sons, 1922 (1st edn. 1912).

Hutchinson, Edward P. *Immigrants and Their Children, 1850-1950.* New York: 1956.

Huthmacher, J. Joseph. *Massachusetts People and Politics, 1919-1933.* Cambridge: Belknap Press of Harvard University, 1959.

Iorizzo, Luciano J. and Mondello, Salvatore. *The Italian-Americans.* Boston: Twayne Publishers, 1971.

Isaacs, Stephen. *Jews and American Politics.* Garden City, New York: Doubleday, 1974.

Jenks, Jeremiah W. and Lauck, W.J. *The Immigration Problem.* New York and London: Funck and Wagnalls Company, 1912.

Jones, Howard Mumford and Jones, Bessie Zabau, eds. *The Many Voices of Boston, A Historical Anthology, 1630-1975.* Boston: Little Brown and Co., 1975.

Joselit, Jenna Weissman. *Our Gang: Jewish Crime and The New York Jewish Community, 1900-1940.* Bloomington: Indiana University Press, 1983.

Joseph, Samuel. *Jewish Immigration to the United States.* New York: Columbia University, 1914.

Kallen, Horace M. *Zionism and World Politics.* Garden City, New York: Doubleday, Page and Company, 1921.

Karp, Abraham J., ed. *The Jewish Experience in America; Selected*

Studies from the Publications of the American Jewish Historical Society. 5 vol. New York: KTAV Publishing House, Inc., 1969.

Kennedy, David M. *Over Here: The First World War and American Society.* New York: Oxford University Press, 1980.

Kessner, Thomas. *The Golden Door: Italian and Jewish Immigrant Mobility in New York City, 1880-1915.* New York: Oxford University Press, 1977.

Kolko, Gabriel. *The Triumph of Conservatism: A Reinterpretation of American History.* New York: Free Press, 1963.

Kramer, Michael S. and Levy, Mark R. *The Ethnic Factor: How America's Minorities Decide Elections.* New York: Simon and Shuster, 1972.

Kraut, Alan M. *The Huddled Masses: The Immigrant in American Society, 1880-1921.* Arlington Heights, Illinois: Harlan Davidson, Inc., 1982.

Kyvig, David E. and Marty, Myron A. *Nearby History: Exploring the Past Around You.* Nashville, Tennessee. The American Association for State and Local History, 1982.

Lenski, Gerhard. *The Religious Factor.* New York: Doubleday & Co., Inc., 1981.

Levin, Murray. *The Complete Politican.* Indianapolis: Bobbs-Merrill, 1962.

Liebman, Arthur. *Jews and the Left.* New York: John Wiley, Sons, 1979.

Lipset, Seymour M. *Political Man: The Social Bases of Politics.* New York: Doubleday & Co., Inc., 1963.

Litt, Edgar. *Beyond Pluralism: Ethnic Politics in America.* Glenview, Illinois: Scott, Foreman, 1970.

Lockard, Duane. *New England State Politics.* Princeton, New Jersey: Princeton University Press, 1959.

Lord, R.H. *History of the Archdiocese of Boston.* New York: Sheed & Ward, 1944.

Lubell, Samuel. *The Future of American Politics.* New York: Harper and Brothers, 1951.

Luce, Robert. *Legislative Assemblies.* Boston: Houghton, Mifflin Company, 1924.

Luce, Robert. *Legislative Principles.* Boston: Houghton, Mifflin Company, 1930.

Luce, Robert. *Legislative Procedures.* Boston: Houghton, Mifflin Company, 1922.

Luce, Robert. *Legislative Problems.* Boston: Houghton, Mifflin Company, 1935.

Mann, Arthur. *Yankee Reformers in an Urban Age.* Cambridge: Belknap Press of Harvard University Press, 1954.

Mann, Arthur, ed. *The Progressive Era: Liberal Renaissance or Liberal Failure.* New York: Holt, Reinhardt, and Winston, 1963.

Marcus, Jacob, ed. *Critical Studies in American Jewish History: Selected Articles from American Jewish Archives.* 3 vol. New York: KTAV Publishing House, Inc., 1971.

Marsden, George M. *Fundamentalism and American Culture: The Shaping of the Twentieth Century Evangelicalism, 1870-1925.* New York: Oxford University Press, 1980.

Mayer, Egon. *From Suburb to Shtetl: The Jews of Bovo Park.* Philadelphia: Temple University Press, 1979.

Memorial of the Celebration of the Two Hundred and Fiftieth Anniversary of the Incorporation of the Town of Malden, Massachusetts, May, 1899. Cambridge: The University Press, 1900.

McCall, Samuel Walker. *Patriotism of the American Jew.* New York: Plymouth Press, Inc., 1924.

McQuade, Vincent A. *The American Catholic Attitude on Child Labor Since 1891.* Washington, D.C.: Catholic University Press, 1938.

Monkkonen, Eric. *Police in Urban America, 1860-1920.* New York: Cambridge University Press, 1981.

Moore, Deborah Dash. *At Home in America: Second Generation*

New York Jews. New York: Columbia University Press, 1981.

Mowry, George. *The California Progressives.* Berkley: 1951.

Paul, Eliot. *Linden on the Saugus Branch.* New York: Random House, 1947.

Perrett, Geoffrey. *America in the Twenties: A History.* New York: Simon and Schuster, 1982.

Plesur, Milton. *Jewish Life in Twentieth Century America: Challenge and Accomodation.* Chicago: Nelson-Hall, 1982.

Porter, Kirk H. and Johnson, Donald B., compilers. *National Party Platforms, 1840-1964.* Urbana: University of Illinois Press, 1966.

Powers, Samuel Leland. *Portraits of a Half Century.* Boston: Little, Brown and Company, 1925.

Rees, Albert. *Real Wages in Manufacturing, 1880-1914.* Princeton: Princeton University Press, 1961.

Rischin, Moses. *The Promised City: New York's Jews, 1870-1914.* Cambridge: Harvard University Press, 1962.

Rischin, Moses, ed. *Immigrants and the American Tradition.* Indianapolis: Bobbs-Merrill Company, Inc., 1976.

Rischin, Moses, ed. *The American Gospel of Success: Individualism and Beyond.* Chicago: Quadrangle Books, 1965.

Roberts, Kenneth L. *Concentrated New England: A Sketch of Calvin Coolidge.* Indianapolis: The Bobbs-Merrill Company, 1924.

Roberts, Kenneth L. *Europe's Morning After.* New York: Harper & Brothers Publishers, 1921.

Roberts, Kenneth L. *Why Europe Leaves Home.* Indianapolis: Bobbs-Merrill, 1920.

Rogin, Michael Paul and Shover, John L. *Political Change in California: Critical Elections and Social Movements, 1890-1966.* Westport: 1970.

Rose, Peter, ed. *The Ghetto and Beyond: Essays on Jewish Life in America.* New York: Random House, 1969.

Rosenberg, Stuart E. *The Jewish Community in Rochester, 1843-1925.* New York: The American Jewish Historical Society by Arrangement with Columbia University Press, 1954.

Ross, Edward A. *The Old World and the New.* New York: The Century Company, 1914.

Rothenberg, Stuart and Licht, Eric. *Ethnic Voters and National Issues.* Washington, D.C.: Free Congress Research and Education Foundation, 1982.

Saveth, Edward N. *American Historians and European Immigrants, 1875-1925.* New York: Columbia University Press, 1948.

Shannon, William V. *The American Irish.* New York: Macmillan, 1963.

Sklare, Marshall, ed. *The Jew in American Society.* New York: Behrman House, 1974.

Sklare, Marshall. *The Jewish Community in America.* New York: Behrman House, 1974.

Solomon, Barbara. *Ancestors and Immigrants: A Changing New England Tradition.* Cambridge: Harvard University Press, 1956.

Stack, John F., Jr. *International Conflict in an American City: Boston's Irish, Italians and Jews, 1935-1944.* Westport: Greenwich Press, 1979.

Steel, Ronald. *Walter Lippman and the American Century.* Boston: Atlantic-Little Brown, 1980.

Strum, Philippa. *Louis D. Brandeis: Justice for the People.* Cambridge: Harvard University Press, 1984.

Taylor, Philip. *The Distant Magnet: European Emigration to the U.S.A. New York: Harper and Row, 1971.*

Teller, Judd L. *Strangers and Natives: The Evolution of the American Jew From 1921 to the Present.* New York: Delacorte Press, 1968.

Thernstrom, Stephen. *The Other Bostonians: Poverty and Progress in the American Metropolis, 1880-1970.* Cambridge: Harvard University Press, 1973.

Thernstrom, Stephen and Sennett, Richard. *Nineteenth Century Cities: Essays in the New Urban History.* New Haven: Yale

University Press, 1969.

Trout, Charles H. *Boston: The Great Depression and the New Deal.* New York: Oxford University Press, 1977.

Underwood, Kenneth W. *Protestant and Catholic*: Religion and Social Interaction in an Industrial Community. Boston: Beacon Press, 1957.

Urofsky, Melvin I. *Louis Brandeis and the Progressive Tradition.* Boston: Little, Brown, 1981.

Wayman, Dorothy G. *David I. Walsh, Citizen-Patriot.* Milwaukee: Bruce Publishing Company, 1952.

Weibe, Robert H. *The Search for Order, 1877-1920.* New York: Hill and Wang, 1967.

Weyle, Nathaniel. *Jews in American Politics.* New Rochelle, N.Y.: Arlington House, 1968.

Wirth, Louis. *The Ghetto.* Chicago: The University of Chicago Press, 1956. (1st edn., 1928)

Wischnitzer, Markus. *To Dwell in Safety: The Story of the Jewish Migration Since 1800.* Philadelphia: Jewish Publication Society of America, 1948.

Wittke, Carl. *We Who Built America: The Saga of the Immigrant.* Cleveland: Western Reserve University Press, 1964. (originally published 1939)

Woods, Robert A., ed. *Americans in Process.* Boston: Houghton, Mifflin and Company, 1902.

Secondary Sources

Articles

Abrams, Richard. "A Paradox of Progressivism," *Political Science Quarterly* (Sept. 1960): 382-385.

Barrows, Robert G. "Beyond the Tenement: Patterns of American Urban Housing, 1870-1930," *Journal of Urban History*, Vol. 9, No.4 (August, 1983): 395-420.

Blackwelder, Julia Kirk. "Crime, Policing, and the Dangerous Classes,"

Journal of Urban History Vol. 10, No. 3 (May, 1984): 329-337.

Blodgett, Geoffrey. "Yankee Leadership in a Divided City, Boston, 1860-1910." *Journal of Urban History. Vol. 8, No. 4 (August, 1982): 371-396.*

Braeman, John. "Seven Progressives," *Business History Review* XXXV (Winter, 1961): 581-192.

Buenker, John D. "The Mahatma and Progressive Reform: Martin Lomasney as Lawmaker, 1911-1917." *New England Quarterly* (September, 1971): 397-419.

Buenker, Jonn D. "The Progressive Era: A Search for a Synthesis." *Mid-America* 51 (July 1969): 175-93.

Gerber, David A. "Cutting out Shylock: Elite Anti-Semitism and the Quest for Moral Order in the Mide-Nineteenth Century American Market Place." *Journal of American History* Vol. 69, No. 3 (December, 1982): 615-637.

Goldstein, Alice. "The Coordinated Use of Data Sources in Research on the Demographic Characteristics and Behavior of Jewish Immigrants to the United States." *American Jewish History* (March, 1983): 293-308.

Greenbaum, Alfred Abraham. "The Early 'Russian' Congregation in America in Its Ethnic and Relgious Setting," *American Jewish Historical Quarterly*, Vol. LXII, No. 2 (December, 1972): 162-170.

Grinnel, Frank. "The Current Controversy About Juries," *Massachusetts Law Quarterly*, Vol. 8 (Nov. 1922-August, 1923): 31-50.

Hayes, Samuel P. "The Politics of Reform in Municipal Government in the Progressive Era." *Pacific Northwest Quarterly* 55 (October 1964).

Hingham, John. "Another Look at Nativsm," *Catholic Historical Review* XLIV (1958-9): 147-58.

Huthmacher, John J. "Urban Liberalism and the Age of Reform." *Mississippi Valley Historical Review* XLIX (September, 1962): 231-41.

Huthmacher, John J. "Charles E. Hughes and Charles F. Murphy:

The Metamorphoses of Progressivism." *New York History* (January, 1965): 25-40.

Jonas, Franklin. "From Russia to America: B. Charney Vladek and the Evolution of Jewish Socialism." In *The American Jewish Experience* 1, ed. Jacob R. Marcus and Abraham Peck. Cincinnati, *American Jewish Archives* (1981) 22-44.

Juliani, Richard. "The Settlement House and the Italian Family," in *The Italian Immigrant Woman in North America. Proceeding of the Tenth Annual Conference of the American Italian Historical Association in conjunction with the Canadian Italian Historical Association,* edited by Betty B. Caroli, Robert F. Harvey, and Lydia F. Toures: (The Multicultural History Society Of Ontario, Toronto, 1978): 103-123.

Kahan, Arcadius. "Economic Choice and Opportunities: The Jewish Immigrant, 1880-1914." *Journal of Economic History* Vol. 38 (1978): 235-251.

Kirshner, Don S. "The Ambiguous Legacy: Social Justice and Social Control in the Progressive Era," *Historical Reflections*, 2 (1975): 69-88.

Kuznets, Simon. "Immigration of Russian Jews to the United States: Background and Structure." *Perspectives in American History* 9 (1975): 35-126.

"Massachusetts and the Foreigner," *New England Magazine* 33 (February, 1906): 726-727.

Monkkonen, Eric H. "The Organized Response to Crime in Nineteenth- and Twentieth-Century America." *The Journal of Interdisciplinary History* Vol. XIV, No. 1 (Summer, 1983): 113-128.

O'Leary, Robert. "Brahmins and Bullyboys: William Henry Cardinal O'Connell and Massachusetts Politics." *Historical Journal of Massachusetts* Vol. X, No. 1 (January, 1982): 3-19.

Perlmann, Joel. "Beyond New York: The Occupations of Russian Jewish Immigrants in Providence, R.I. and Other Small Jewish

Communities, 1900-1915." *American Jewish History* (March, 1983): 369-394.

Putnam, Frank. "Massachusetts in an Era of Industrial Prosperity and Political Buncombe." *New England Magazine* 37 (December 1907): 395-418 .

Ross, Edward A. "Racial Consequences in Immigration." *The Century Magazine* LXXXVII (February, 1914): 616, 621.

Schneider, William, Berman, Michael D., Schultz, Mark. "Bloc Voting Reconsidered: Is There a Jewish Vote?" *Ethnicity* No. 4 (December, 1974): 364.

Sherman, Richard B. "Charles Sumner Bird and the Progressive Party in Massachusetts." *New England Quarterly* 33 (September 1960): 325-340.

Sherman, Richard B. "Foss of Massachusetts -- Demagogue or Progressive?" *Mid-America* 43 (April 1961): 75-94.

Sherman, Richard B. "The Status Revolution and Massachusetts Progressive Leadership." *Political Science Quarterly* 78 (1913): 59-65.

Solomon, Barbara M. "The Intellectual Background of the Immigrant Restriction Movement in New England." *New England Quarterly* 25 (March 1952): 47-59.

Swierenja, Robert. "Ethnicultural Political Analysis: A New Approach to American Ethnic Studies." *Journal of American Studies* 5 (April 1971): 59-79.

Thelan, David P. "Social Tension and the Origins of Progressivism." *Journal of American History* 56 (September 1969): 323-41.

Toll, William. "The Female Life Cycle and the Measure of Social Change: Portland, Oregon, 1880-1930." *American Jewish History* (March, 1983): 309-332.

Watts, Eugene J. "Police Response to Crime and Disorder in Twentieth-Century St. Louis." *The Journal of American History* Vol. 70, No. 2 (September, 1983): 340-358.

Weinberg, Daniel E. "Viewing the Immigrant Experience in American Through Fiction and Autobiography -- with a Select Bibliography." *The History Teacher* (May, 1976): 409-432.

Wyman, Roger E. "Middle-Class Voters and Progressive Reform: The Conflicts of Class and Culture." *American Political Science Review* 69 (1974): 488-504.

Illustrations

Charts

Figures

Photographs

Index

R

S